THE ITALIAN/AMERICAN EXPERIENCE

A Collection of Writings

Louis J. Gesualdi

University Press of America,® Inc.
Lanham · Boulder · New York · Toronto · Plymouth, UK

Copyright © 2012 by
University Press of America,® Inc.
4501 Forbes Boulevard
Suite 200
Lanham, Maryland 20706
UPA Acquisitions Department (301) 459-3366

10 Thornbury Road
Plymouth PL6 7PP
United Kingdom

Library of Congress Control Number: 2012931972
ISBN: 978-0-7618-5860-7 (paperback : alk. paper)
eISBN: 978-0-7618-5861-4

This book is dedicated to my parents John and Catherine Gesualdi.

CONTENTS

PREFACE

There have been many misperceptions written about Southern Italians and Italian Americans. The purpose of this book is to present research that shows these misperceptions are inaccurate. Also, the purpose of this book is to present sources to help the reader become more cognizant of the Italian American experience.

Chapter 1 shows that the negative notion of Southern Italy devouring the resources of Northern Italy is inaccurate.

In chapters 2 and 3 research is provided that does not support the notion of poverty in Southern Italy being an outcome of family values.

Chapter 4 presents the major problems of an explanation stating Italian Americans are not as successful as other ethnic groups in the United States because of cultural traits brought over from Italy.

In chapter 5 data, indicating that Italian Americans are inaccurately portrayed and misperceived as being involved in criminality and socially undesirable behavior are presented.

Chapter 6 describes research showing that the traditional community life had been of great benefit to the physical and mental health of the Italian Americans living in Roseto, Pennsylvania.

In chapters 7 and 8 Giovanni Schiavo who has written many books on Italian American contribution to the development of the United States is discussed.

Chapter 9 suggests the kind of research involving the Italian American experience that is needed.

In chapters 10 and 11 resources are provided for persons interested in studying the Italian American experience.

It is my wish that these 11 chapters will stimulate a desire by the reader to become more interested in ethnic studies.

Louis Gesualdi, Ph.D. St. John's University

ACKNOWLEDGMENTS

I wish to thank Kathleen V. MacDonald, Dean of the College of Professional Studies, St. John's University, for her support and assistance that enabled me to write this book. Second, I would like to indicate my gratitude to Tom Ward, Associate Professor of Criminal Justice, St. John's University, for his many suggestions and advice over the years. Third, I wish to thank George Hoffecker for our many conversations on ethnic stereotyping that provided me with valuable information for the completion of my book. Fourth, I would like to thank Francis A. Lees, Professor of Economics and Finance, St. John's University, for his suggestion to write a guide on Italian/American studies that became chapter 10 of this book. Fifth, I would like to indicate my gratitude to Laura Espinoza for editing my book. Sixth, I am very grateful to Jo Mauro for all the help and guidance that she has given me in the last twenty-five years. Finally, I wish to thank Lisa Kuan, my fiancée, for typesetting my book and for her assistance and moral encouragement.

INTRODUCTION

It is important that Italian Americans (as well as other groups) are familiar with their own group's experience and to grasp what is considered productive and practical to shaping their lives. The collection of writings (nine of the eleven were previously published) chosen for this publication, hopefully, will be a meaningful beginning for Italian Americans to become informed of their group's experience. This publication contains works showing how popular negative notions of Italian/American life are inaccurate. Moreover, it contains writings that provide useful information on Italian American heritage.

The first work "An Inaccurate Notion of Southern Italy" demonstrates that the negative notion of Southern Italy, devouring the resources of Northern Italy, is incorrect. It is shown that the Northern region of Italy, historically, has benefited greatly from the Southern region.[1]

Second, "A Reply to *The Moral Basis of a Backward Society*" is a response to Edward C. Banfield's book *The Moral Basis of a Backward Society*. This essay is an attempt to take into account some of the major criticisms pertaining to Banfield's work during the past forty years.[2]

Third, "*Making Democracy Work:* Criticisms and Response" is a response to Robert D. Putnam's study. It is an attempt to discuss some of the major criticisms concerning Putnam's book.[3]

Fourth, "The Cultural Trait Approach: A Critique" briefly reviews some of the research on the cultural trait approach. It presents briefly some of the major problems and weaknesses of this viewpoint by analyzing some of the overall studies on the educational and occupational achievements of different ethnic groups and by examining the historical migration patterns of these groups.[4]

Fifth, "Popular Held Belief about Italian Americans and Organized Crime" demonstrates that the commonly held belief about Italian Americans and organized crime is not true. It presents social scientific studies indicating that Italian Americans did not develop organized crime in the United States.[5]

Sixth, "Bruhn and Wolf's Study of Roseto, Pennsylvania: A Brief Discussion" discusses John G. Bruhn and Stewart Wolf's book *The Roseto Story: An*

Anatomy of Health. It indicates that a close knit community (such as the Italian American community of Roseto) acts as an area of defense against the effects of stress, bereavement and life changes.[6]

Seventh, "Giovanni Schiavo's Works: A Summary" sums up Schiavo's key studies. This essay concludes that the reading of Giovanni Schiavo's books is a significant beginning to an awareness of the Italian American experience.[7]

Eighth, "Praises for Giovanni Schiavo" documents the praises by many scholars and writers for Schiavo's contribution to Italian American studies.[8]

Ninth, "Some Ideas for Italian/American Research in the Twenty-first Century" presents some ideas for research that may be useful for Italian Americans to become aware of their group's history.[9]

Tenth, "Italian American Studies: A Guide" is a resource for persons interested in studying the Italian American experience. This chapter lists a number of organizations and journal specializing in Italian American culture and it provides a brief description of many leading researchers in the field of Italian American studies.[10]

Finally, "The Italian American Experience: An Annotated Bibliography" is an annotated bibliography of some key books dealing with the lives of Italians and Italian Americans. It is a resource for persons interested in studying the Italian/American experience.[11]

The eleven works are an introduction to an understanding of Italian/American social and economic life. It is this author's wish that this publication will stimulate a desire by the reader to become more interested in becoming knowledgeable of the ethnic group experience in the United States.

NOTES

1. Gesualdi, Louis, "An Inaccurate Notion of Southern Italy," *ComUnico Magazine,* June 2000.

2. Gesualdi, Louis, *A Reply to the Moral Basis of a Backward Society,* New York, NY: John D. Calandra Topical Issues Series of City University of New York, 2001.

3. Gesualdi, Louis, "Making Democracy Work: Criticisms and Response" in Jerome Krase, Philip Cannistraro and Joseph Scelsa (editors), *Italian American Politics: Local, Global/Cultural, Personal,* Staten Island, NY: American Italian Historical Association, 2005.

4. Gesualdi, Louis, *The Cultural Trait Approach: A Critique,* New York, NY: John D. Calandra Topical Issues Series at City University New York, 2001.

5. Gesualdi, Louis, "Popular Held Beliefs about Italian Americans and Organized Crime" (unpublished paper), 2006.

6. Gesualdi, Louis, "Bruhn and Wolf's Study of Roseto, Pennsylvania: A Brief Discussion," *ComUnico Magazine,* October, 2000.

7. Gesualdi, Louis, "Giovanni Schiavo's Works: A Summary," *ComUnico Magazine,* February 2000.

8. Gesualdi, Louis, "Praises for Giovanni Schiavo," *ComUnico Magazine,* October 2000.

9. Gesualdi, Louis, "Some Ideas for Italian American Research" presented at *The Italian American Experience in the New York City Area Conference,"* Jamaica, NY: Italian Cultural Center of St. John's University, September 28, 2001.

10. Gesualdi, Louis, *Italian American Studies: A Guide*, Global Monograph Series, No.11, Center for Global Education, Jamaica, NY: St. John's University, March 1999.

11. Gesualdi, Louis, *The Italian American Experience: An Annotated Bibliography*, Voices in Italian Americana Internet Site, 2005.

CHAPTER 1

AN INACCURATE NOTION OF SOUTHERN ITALY[1]

A negative notion of the Southern region of Italy has been that this region, historically, absorbed or devoured the resources of the more economically advanced Northern region of Italy. Antonio Gramsci in *The Southern Question*[1] provides evidence that does not support this notion.

1. At the end of the nineteenth century and at the beginning of the twentieth century, a great deal of industrialization (leading to large amounts of resources) developed in Northern Italy. Gramsci pointed out that this industrialization would not have been possible without Southern Italy. He explained that Southern Italy provided the badly needed labor force for the Northern industries, and that without this labor force, Northern Italy could not have generated great amounts of resources.[2]

2. Almost eighty percent of the millions of Italian immigrants who arrived in America from 1880 to 1920 originally came from Southern Italy. Gramsci explained that the money that these immigrants sent to their families in Southern Italy was key in the development of industrialization in Northern Italy. During that time period, the Italian government offered treasury bonds with guaranteed interest and many Italian immigrants in America with their families in Southern Italy invested in these bonds. This money, as noted by Gramsci, was used by the Italian government to provide the financial means to subsidize the industries of Northern Italy. Moreover, Gramsci pointed out that millions of dollars of Southern Italians' bank savings were invested in promoting businesses in Northern

Italy. Thus, Southern Italy did not absorb the resources of Northern Italy but actually helped to produce these resources.[3]

After examining Gramsci's *The Southern Question,* it is obvious that the Northern region of Italy, historically, has benefited greatly from the Southern region. Southern Italy has provided a great deal of the labor and money in the development of industries in Northern Italy.[4] In conclusion, the negative notion of Southern Italy, devouring the resources of Northern Italy, is inaccurate.

NOTES

1. Originally published in *ComUnico Magazine,* June 2000.
2. Gramsci, Antonio, *The Southern Question,* Toronto, ON: Guernica Editions, Inc., 1995.
3. Ibid.
4. Ibid.

CHAPTER 2

A REPLY TO *THE MORAL BASIS OF A BACKWARD SOCIETY*[1]

Edward C. Banfield, in *The Moral Basis of a Backward Society*, described a Southern Italian community, Montegrano, in which the people of this town were shown to be unwilling to involve themselves in any public problem or activity outside the nuclear family. He also portrayed these people to be self-serving and shortsighted in their behavior. To explain such behavior, Banfield hypothesized that the Italians from Southern Italy had the following family value: "Maximize the material, short-run material advantage of the nuclear family, assume that all others will do likewise." In other words, Southern Italians valued mistrusting people outside the nuclear family. Banfield called this value amoral familism. He stated that the poverty in Southern Italy was the result of this mistrust value.[2]

The Moral Basis of a Backward Society, unfortunately, has been influential in the study of Italians and Italian-Americans by many social scientists of today, and it has been, intentionally or unintentionally, used to inaccurately characterize Italians and Italian-Americans in a pessimistic and stereotypical way. Banfield's influence can be seen in many successful works on Southern Italy and the Italian American community (see works by Herbert Gans,[3] Gerald D. Suttles,[4] Humbert Nelli,[5] and Robert Putnam[6]).

This chapter is a reply to E. C. Banfield's study. It is an attempt to take into account some of the major criticisms pertaining to Banfield's book over the last forty years. Since Banfield's work has been influential in portraying Italians and Italian-Americans in such a negative way, an examination of some these criticisms would be valuable in order to describe this ethnic group accurately.

Let's look at the criticisms involving the value "amoral familism" that have been published in reviews, articles and books.

Thomas McCorkel in his review of *The Moral Basis of a Backward Society* remarked that the presence of "amoral familism" was documented by Banfield partly through field observations and partly by way of explanation of the answer of thirty-one individuals to only a single Thematic Apperception Test picture. He pointed out that Banfield contrasted Southern Italy with Utah without satisfactory handling of the histories of the two areas. No attention, according to McCorkel, was given by Banfield that "amoral familism" may have been a piece of a formation that made up a favorable acclimatization to a political atmosphere that hindered formal organizations of all types. Furthermore, McCorkel suggested that *The Moral Basis of a Backward Society* would have been a more valuable study if Banfield had discussed leader-follower cases in family or informal (such as hunting and café) organizations or all three.[7]

Joseph Lopreato in *Peasants No More* analyzed social change in Southern Italy as an effect of emigration, disagreeing with Banfield's account of "amoral familism." Lopreato found Banfield's study in essence ahistorical. He pointed out that Banfield was extremely hasty to attribute causality for what were in actuality the outcomes or characteristics of a very extended complicated and on weak foundation when he stated that the people of Montegrano lacked a vitality of motivation. As Lopreato noted, Southern Italy, a country of peasants, was really not suitable to agriculture. He demonstrated that in Southern Italy the most painstaking work very often came to naught and did nothing to eliminate deep-seated set of facts. Lopreato maintained that one can agree fundamentally with Banfield's simple report of the facts, but only to the magnitude that it was meant to be relevant to the most poverty-stricken segment of the peasantry- rather than to the category as a totality. Banfield, according to Lopreato, was the secular misery. Moreover, he brought attention to the fact that in those few instances in which cooperative enterprises were undertaken by the Southern Italian peasants, they were, immediately without fail, cheated.[8]

Sydel F. Silverman compared and contrasted her research in Central Italy with Banfield's study in Southern Italy. She accepted Banfield's description of Southern Italian behavior as accurate and that an amoral familistic rule existed. However, she pointed out that Banfield failed to provide an explanation for the existence of amoral familism. Silverman argued that economic and social conditions created and maintained value systems, such as amoral familism, and that values were not the principal factor in explaining behavioral characteristics. She stated that values were more a dependent than an independent factor.[9]

N. S. Peabody in his essay "Toward an Understanding of Backwardness and Change: A Critique of the Banfield Hypothesis" studied in detail Banfield's amoral familism and examined other works that dealt with the history of the Mezzogiorno (Southern Italy). He rejected the validity of Banfield's prediction about socioeconomic change in the Mezzogiorno, and showed that Southern Italy was modernizing regardless of the existence of amoral familism. Peabody pointed out that the interaction patterns had stayed by all means constant and that a collective endeavor had no real part in the development of the Mezzogiorno. Finally, he explained the reality of amoral familism as a pragmatic response to life in a hopelessly severe and unpredictable environment. Peabody in disagreement with Banfield asserted that amoral familism was the result of stagnant surroundings not the reason for its stagnation. He concluded that Banfield's interpretation of Southern Italy's poverty was both irrelative and wrong.[10]

J. Davis in his essay "Morals and Backwardness" indicated that for amoral familism to explain anything, Banfield would have had to show that the Montegranesi consciously applied this value in their behavior. This, according to Davis, Banfield did not do. Furthermore, Davis mentioned that it was unknown for moral principles to stand up on their own against economic benefit. He stated that an explanation (in this case amoral familism) which presumed this, confused behaviors with ideas to the loss of examination and prediction. Davis argued that moral ideas constantly gave way to economic possibility. Thus, Davis' reasoning, in disagreement to Banfield's interpretation, was that one needed to look at the control on actions and outcomes of actions before presupposing the predominant influence of moral ideas on actions and decisions.[11]

William Muraskin in his article "The Moral Basis of a Backward Sociologist: Edward Banfield, the Italians and the Italian-Americans" demonstrated that Banfield, determined to support a psychological interpretation of social behavior rather than a socioeconomic one, made statements and conclusions that were highly questionable. He showed that Banfield's own data contradicted his amoral familism explanation of the poverty situation in Southern Italy. Muraskin, through the use of Banfield's own observations, established that the Italians of Montegrano lived in a harsh economic and social environment, and pointed out that their labors were exploited by the upper class. In conclusion, Muraskin explained that the Southern Italians did not value nor had a psychological need to mistrust outsiders, but that they saw no other choices, and that while these Italians probably desired the values of cooperation and trust, they had set these values aside for a more practical value.[12]

Jane and Peter Schneider in their book *Culture and Political Economy in Western Sicily* explained the role of Sicily in historical world-systems and examined its consequences for the cultural values of the region. Their work investigated Sicily's role in the post industrialization world system of the nineteenth and twentieth centuries, and it indicated that as an outcome of this system the farmers of Sicily moved from producing and exporting food to exporting human labor. Their conclusions about the role of culture in Southern Italy were different from Banfield's conclusions. Cultural values, as shown by the Schneiders, were the outcomes of a society's position in a world-system that was based on dominant and subordinate relationships. The Schneiders stated that culture helped distinct groups to claim certain power and that when a cultural value, such as amoral familism, appeared to hinder progress, it was because certain interest groups benefit in resisting key changes and were managing cultural values to do so.[13]

Leonard W. Moss in his article "The Family in Southern Italy: Yesterday and Today" pointed out that although to some degree there was a practice of amoral familism by the farmers in Southern Italy, Banfield's conclusion about a complete lack of communal cooperation by the Southern Italians was incorrect. Moss noted that Banfield's work missed certain community enterprises that existed in Southern Italy, such as godparent relationships, patron-client relations, trade networks, peer groups and circles of intimacy among friends. The misrepresentations, according to Moss, which developed in *The Moral Basis of a Backward Society* can be explained by the fact that Banfield's knowledge of the Italian language was simple and that he was aided in his research in Southern Italy by his wife Laura Fasano Banfield, whose parents came from Northern Italy (hostility existed between Northern Italians and Southern Italians).[14]

Richard Alba in his book *Italian Americans Into the Twilight of Ethnicity* did not support Banfield's notion that Southern Italy's poverty was the result of the value amoral familism. Alba pointed out that families in Southern Italy were not so commonly separated (that is, were not so mistrustful of outsiders). He noted ways in which families in Southern Italy united with one another to strengthen their social positions. These ways involved linking families and individuals through kinship, marriage, godparentship and friendship.[15]

Frank A. Salamone in his article "Moral Familism: Italian-Americans and Societa" questioned the existence of the value amoral familism in Southern Italy. In refuting Banfield's work, Salamone showed Southern Italians adhering to groups beyond the nuclear family and setting up networks that were useful in coping with a hostile environment. He also demonstrated that the Italians from Southern Italy were not short-sighted and self-serving in their behavior.[16]

Richard Gambino in his article "America's Most Tolerated Intolerance: Bigotry against Italian Americans" suggested that Banfield's hypothesis of Southern Italians having an amoral familism value was incorrect. Gambino pointed out that Southern Italians did involve themselves in activities outside the nuclear family. He explained that the family system of Southern Italy was one of extended families. These extended families were linked beyond blood both by arranged marriages and by a system of godparenthood that developed into an elaborate network or a community system.[17]

In general, the criticisms that have been levied against Banfield attacked his work on two general counts. There were insufficiencies in his description and weaknesses in his analysis. These critics took the position that a value could not be regarded as a cause or satisfactory explanation of behavior. Overall, the criticisms and facts did not support Banfield's argument concerning the family values of Southern Italians. Southern Italian culture was not the cause of its poverty, but was on the contrary a consequence and a means of adapting to it.

It is this author's opinion that Banfield's description of the environment that the Southern Italians were living under in Montegrano was valid. One can essentially agree with Banfield's description of the facts, but only to the extent that it was meant to apply to economically underprivileged Southern Italians rather than to the whole Southern Italian peasantry (see Lopreato[18]). The value concerning a mistrust of people outside the family was a pragmatic response to life hopelessly harsh and uncertain environment. This author (in agreement with Silverman[19]) argues that economic and social conditions create and maintain value systems and that values are not the primary element in cultivating or hindering changes or in explaining behavioral characteristics. Values are more a dependent than independent variable.

In conclusion, this author argues that in order to understand the social realities of Southern Italians and Italian-Americans (for that matter any ethnic group), it is important to investigate social and economic factors outside the family circle. It has been too common for researchers, such as Banfield, to examine only the family values of a group and not the factors that create or help maintain these values. Economic and social factors create and maintain a value system, such as amoral familism, and that a value is not the predominant reason in explaining a group's behavior. The amoral familism value was not a satisfactory explanation for the poverty that existed (and still exists) in Southern Italy. Amoral familism was the result of an impoverished society and not a cause of its impoverishment.

NOTES

1. Originally published as a booklet by the John D. Calandra Topical Issues Series, John D. Calandra Institute, City University of New York, New York, NY: 2001.

2. Banfield, Edward C., *The Moral Basis of a Backward Society,* New York, NY: The Free Press, 1958.

3. Gans, Herbert, *The Urban Villagers: Group and Class in the Life of Italian–Americans,* New York,NY: The Free Press, 1962.

4. Suttles, Gerald D., *The Social Order of a Slum: Ethnicity and Territory in the Inner City,* Chicago, IL: University of Chicago Press, 1968.

5. Humbert Nelli, *The Italians in Chicago, 1880–1930,* New York, NY: Oxford University Press, 1970.

6. Putnam, Robert, *Making Democracy Work: Civic Traditions in Modern Italy,* Princeton, NJ: Princeton University Press, 1993.

7. McCorkel, Thomas, "Review of *The Moral Basis of a Backward Society* by E. C. Banfield," *American Anthropologist,* 61, 1959.

8. Lopreato, Joseph, *Peasants No More,* Scranton, PA: Chandler Publishing, Co., 1967.

9. Silverman, Sydel F., "Agricultural Organization, Social Structure and Values in Italy: Amoral Familism Reconsidered," *American Anthropologist,* Vol. LXX, No. 1, 1968, 1–20.

10. Peabody, N. S., "Toward an Understanding of Backwardness and Change: A Critique of the Banfield Hypothesis," *The Journal of Developing Areas,* 4, 1970.

11. Davis, J., "Morals and Backwardness," *Comparative Studies in Society and History, 12,* 1970.

12. Muraskin, William, "The Moral Basis of a Backward Sociologist: Edward Banfield," *American Journal of Sociology, 20,* 1974.

13. Schneider, Jane and Peter, *Culture and Political Economy in Western Sicily,* New York, NY: Academia Press, 1976.

14. Moss, Leonard W., "The Family in Southern Italy: Yesterday and Today" in H. S. Nelli (editor), *The United States and Italy: The First Two Hundred Years,* Staten Island, NY: American Italian Historical Association, 1977.

15. Alba, Richard, *Italian Americans into the Twilight of Ethnicity,* Englewood Cliffs, NJ: Prentice–Hall, Inc., 1985.

16. Salamone, Frank A., "Moral Basis: Italian–Americans and Society" in R. N. Juliani and S. P. Juliani (editors), *New Exploration in Italian American Studies,* Staten Island, NY: American Italian Historical Association, 1994.

17. Gambino, Richard, "America's Most Tolerated Intolerance: Bigotry against Italian Americans," *The Italian American Review,* Volume 6, Number 1, 1997.

18. Lopreato, *Peasants No More,* 1967.

19. Silverman, "Agricultural Organization, Social Structure and Values in Italy: Amoral Familism Reconsidered," 1968.

CHAPTER 3

MAKING DEMOCRACY WORK: CRITICISMS AND RESPONSE[1]

Robert D. Putnam in *Making Democracy Work: Civic Traditions in Modern Italy* investigates the attitudes and the economic situation of Southern Italians in Italy during the 1970s and the 1980s. His book states that, in general, a culture of trust fosters a higher degree of social integration and political/economic development than it's opposite. It argues that mutual trust and civic involvement make economic prosperity. The author contends that the successful communities in Northern and Central Italy became well off mainly because of the people's high levels of trust and civic engagement. He maintains that in the 1970s and 1980s Southern Italy's lack of political/economic development and its high levels of poverty were the outcomes of this region's long history of low levels of trust and civic involvement.[2]

This chapter is a response to Robert D. Putnam's study. It is an attempt to discuss some of the major criticisms concerning Putnam's book. *Making Democracy Work* has received much attention from policy makers and civic activists in America and around the world. It was the winner of the 1993 Brownlow Book Award of the National Academy of Public Administration. Since *Making Democracy Work* has received such attention, a discussion of some of the criticisms of this work would be valuable for future research dealing with Italian and/or Italian-American politics.

M. L. Mannin in his critique of *Making Democracy Work* contests the information of Putnam's work. He points out problems in Putnam's book that involve an over dependence on information from Italy's elite and a historical summary of Italy not containing any description of the fascist period. Mannin further states that Putnam's study fails in the following two ways. First, as an addition to inquiry regarding organizational efficiency, its small empirical foundation (that is, small sample size of councilor surveys) is inappropriate for the extended contribution that it proclaims to make to a democratic viewpoint. Second, Putnam in his study neglects to reveal the dishonesty within those very regions in Northern and Central Italy that are held as sparkling examples of successful democratic activity. He declines to report the lack of competent democratic liability and the deficiency of civic engagement in Northern Italy and Central Italy as well as Southern Italy over the past forty years.[3]

Marco Maraffi in his review indicates that *Making Democracy Work* can be scrutinized in a number of ways. First, an association between variables (such as high levels of trust and economic prosperity) does not prove causality (as it is argued in Putnam's work). Second, Putnam's discussion over long periods of time of low levels of trust and civic involvement in Southern Italy is not developed very well.[4]

Nadia Urbinati in her review presents the following criticisms to *Making Democracy Work*. First, Putnam's conclusion would suggest that where a culture of civic distinction is not current, good democratic organizations, then, cannot be developed. In other words, according to Putnam, there is little room for human decision, and, above all, for political action. Urbinati argues that an area is not permanently barred from enjoying democratic organizations because such organizations did not exist in its history. Second, Urbinati explains that the development of contemporary political life in Italy contradicts Putnam's interpretation. For instance, she notes that even in Southern Italy, civil society is demonstrating its will to change the rules that have regulated its citizens during the last decades. Her review demonstrates that the residents of Southern Italy, for the first time in their history, have smashed through the impenetrability of omerta (the Mafia's code of silence). These residents have established protest movements against corrupt governmental administration, and they are making demands for major governmental changes.[5]

In general, the criticisms that have been levied against Putnam attack his work on two general counts. First, there are insufficiencies in description and weaknesses in his analysis. Second, Putnam does not successfully show that Southern Italy's culture is the cause of its high levels of poverty.

It is my opinion, that Putnam's description of the different levels of trust and civic participation in regions of Northern, Central and Southern Italy is valid. I argue that high levels of trust and civic participation are associated (correlated) with political and economic development. However, correlation is not a causal explanation. No serious consideration was given by Putnam concerning the low levels of trust and lack of civic participation as being a part of a configuration that constitutes a successful adaptation to a political climate that discourages participation in formal associations of all varieties. *Making Democracy Work* would have been a better book if Putnam had examined other types of participation by Southern Italians. These would include leader-follower patterns in family and informal groups, such as hunting and café.[6] Finally, Putnam needed to incorporate in his book such studies as: Joseph Lopreato's *Peasant's*

No More[7], Sydel Silverman's "Agricultural Organization, Social Structure and Values in Italy: Amoral Familism Reconsidered"[8] and Jane and Peter Schneider's *Culture and Political Economy in Western Sicily.*[9] These works would have provided Putnam with a much better understanding of the history of Southern Italy and how economic factors influence levels of trust.

NOTES

1. Originally published in Krase, Jerome Cannistraro Philip, and Scelsa, Joseph (editors), *Italian American Politics: Local, Global/Cultural, Personal*, Staten Island, NY: American Italian Historical Association, 2005.

2. Putnam, Robert D., *Making Democracy Work: Civic Traditions in Modern Italy*, Princeton, NJ: Princeton University Press, 1993.

3. Mannin, M. L., "European Politics–*Making Democracy Work*," *Political Studies*, September 1994, p. 533.

4. Maraffi, Marco, "Review of *Making Democracy Work*," *American Journal of Sociology*, March 1999, pp. 1348–1349.

5. Urbinati, Nadia, "The Art of Tolerance–*Making Democracy Work*," *Dissent*, Fall 1993, pp. 572–573.

6. See McCorkel, Thomas, "Review of *The Moral Basis of a Backward Society* by E.C. Banfield," *American Anthropologist*, 61, 1959.

7. Lopreato, Joseph, *Peasants No More*, Scranton, PA: Chandler Publishing Co., 1967.

8. Silverman, Sydel F., "Agricultural Organization, Social Structure and Values in Italy: Amoral Familism Reconsidered," *American Anthropologist*, Vol. LXX, No. 1, 1968.

9. Schneider, Jane and Peter, *Culture and Political Economy in Western Sicily*, New York, NY: Academia Press, 1976.

CHAPTER 4

THE CULTURAL TRAIT APPROACH: A CRITIQUE[1]

In an attempt to understand and explain various characteristics of the different immigrant groups in the United States many researchers from the 1950s to the 1990s have argued that an ethnic group's adjustment to a country may be understood by the continuities it shows with its past. For example, it has been stated that immigrant or ethnic groups maintain specific practices and attitudes of their ancestors. In other words, aspects of the present day behavior of ethnic groups are principally the outcomes of enduring norms, values and attitudes brought over to America from their country of origin[2]. This explanation is referred to as the cultural trait approach. Cultural traits are defined as norms, values and attitudes which were developed in the ethnic group's country of origin and maintained by the group in the United States.[3] This chapter briefly reviews some of the research on the cultural trait approach and presents the major problems and weaknesses of this viewpoint by analyzing some of the overall studies on the educational and occupational achievements of different ethnic groups (specifically Italian, Jewish, Irish and Asian Americans) and by examining the historical migration patterns of these groups. The historical migration patterns, that are discussed in this study involve: 1) the time period of the immigrant or ethnic group's migration to America and the permanency of the migration; and 2) the educational and occupational background of the group before their migration to the United States.

Alfred Kroeber[4], Alfred Kroeber and Talcott Parsons[5], and Talcott Parsons,[6] argued that there is maintenance of cultural traits (that is, values, habits and ideas) among different groups and that these traits are the major factors in explaining behavior. Works by Strodtbeck,[7] Rosen,[8] Gordon,[9] Covello,[10] Glazer and Moynihan,[11] Thernstrom,[12] Greeley and McCready,[13] Gambino,[14] LaGumina and

Cavaioli,[15] Kessner,[16] Briggs,[17] Greeley,[18] Glazer,[19] Egelman,[20] Browne,[21] Oxnam,[22] Graubard,[23] and Sowell [24] have used the cultural trait approach to explain ethnic behavior in America. These authors stated that there is maintenance of cultural values (that is, cultural traits) among the different ethnic groups in the United States. They argued that cultural traits are the major factors in explaining the differences in the educational and occupational achievements in the U. S. of the various ethnic groups.

Fred Strodtbeck in his research compared the Jews and Italians of New Haven in achievement. Strodtbeck stated that Jewish values had always stressed educational and intellectual achievement for their offspring, while the Italian immigrant parent viewed school as an upper class institution which threatened the parents' desire to keep the offspring under the family's control. Family life, according to Strodtbeck, was viewed as more important than schooling by the Italian parent.[25]

Bernard C. Rosen indicated that, compared to other white ethnics, Italian-Americans did not value independent training and motivation and did not encourage their children to achieve educational and occupational success. Among the Italian immigrants, according to Rosen, school learning was not an avenue for socioeconomic advancement for their offspring. Rosen stated that book learning was not part of the everyday Italian experience and that the Italians had a mistrust of intellectualism. He also said that, according to the Italian, only the upper class went to school.[26]

Milton Gordon indicated that Jewish-Americans have enjoyed disproportionate success which can be attributed to the distinctive values that Jews carried over with them as part of their cultural tradition from Europe. Gordon stated that the Jews arrived in America with middle-class values of thrift, sobriety, ambition, desire for education, ability to postpone immediate gratification for the sake of long-range goals, and aversion to violence already internalized. He argued that it was these cultural values which account for the rapid rise of the Jewish group in occupational status and economic affluence.[27]

Leonard Covello stated that education to the Italian parent (that is, the Italian peasant) was the teaching of society's cultural, social and moral values to the child by the parents. The Italian peasant, in order to maintain the Italian way of life, opposed education from outside the family. Covello noted that the Italian's mistrust of school, which developed in Southern Italy and was a noticeable part of the peasant's culture, was maintained in America. This was exemplified by the lack of cordial relations between the American teachers and the Southern Italian parents.[28]

Nathan Glazer and Daniel P. Moynihan noted that Italian American children were not encouraged by their family of origin to achieve educational success as individuals while Jewish American children were strongly encouraged by their families to succeed as individuals. These authors argued that few Italian Americans have achieved educational success as a result of family values. These values were brought over from Italy and maintained in this country.[29]

Stephen Thernstrom indicated a downward socioeconomic trend among Italian and Irish Catholic males that he did not find with other groups in Boston.

Thernstrom stated that, compared to other groups, a higher percentage of first and second generation Italian and Irish American Catholics who moved into white collar occupations returned to blue-collar jobs. He concluded that cultural factors, created and maintained by the Irish and Italian families, led to their different occupational patterns.[30]

Richard Gambino stated that because of their negative attitude toward schooling and their desire to remain close to the family circle (their attitude and desire brought over to America from Italy) Italian Americans have gone into blue-collar rather than white-collar work. He noted that those few Italian Americans who have gone into white-collar work and professional careers have chosen occupations where one's personal accomplishment did not interfere with one's family.[31]

Salvatore LaGumina and Frank Cavaioli, after looking at the experience of a number of different ethnic groups, pointed out that there is a continued presence of ethnic diversity (the maintaining of cultural traits) in the United States. These two authors concluded that "ethnicity persists" and "groups in this country remain distinctive and visible as they meet many individual and social needs."[32]

Andrew Greeley and William McCready, continuing on this theme, argued that there exist ethnic differences in behavior and that the knowledge of a group's heritage (cultural traits) is essential to the understanding of their present economic position and behavior. According to Greeley and McCready, heritage may not explain everything, but it is clear that much cannot be explained without investigating the cultural background of the country of origin.[33]

Thomas Kessner's work *The Golden Door*, a study of Italians and Jews in New York City between 1880 and 1915, indicated that both ethnic groups moved up the occupational ladder but the Italians mostly confined their climb to skilled blue-collar work. Kessner stated that the Italians considered education an unimportant continuation of one's childhood. He commented that the maintenance of this Italian attitude had the following effects on the offspring: the second generation's occupational similarity with their elders, especially in unskilled jobs; the persistence of the offspring in Italian immigrant neighborhoods; the fact that the second generation did not differ much from the first generation in occupational interests; and the fact that participation in American schools by the offspring made no great difference in their occupational viewpoint in comparison with their parents.[34]

John Walker Brigg's account of Italian "colonies" in Utica and Rochester, New York and in Kansas City, Missouri during the years of the Great Migration to America indicated that the Italians had clear cut, preconceived ideas about man and his position in society before they emigrated from Italy and they employed these ideas to good effect in their new environment. Their ideas concerning self-help, group organization, social mobility and the economic value of education, according to Briggs, had been of aid to them in Italy and they proved to be equally useful in America. Briggs stated that once the Italians had made the decision to remain in America rather than return to Italy after having accumulated some money, they set about to succeed in the United States while at the same time retaining their traditions and heritage. Briggs argued that the Italians were believers in social mobility and valued education as an avenue to personal and family betterment and as such fitted in quite well with Americans who had similar if not identical social concepts.[35]

Nathan Glazer looked at the economic success of Jewish Americans and Asian Americans and claimed that their success is based on their educational achievement. Jewish and Asian Americans, according to Glazer, achieved higher success than other groups as a result of their cultural background.[36] He stated:

> If we are interested in raising levels of educational achievement in certain groups (i.e., ethnic groups who do not achieve well in school or assimilate easily) it seems reasonable to assume that social and cultural factors that hamper educational achievement may be more accessible to policy intervention.[37]

Glazer believed that the reason the Jews and Asians succeeded in America is that they possessed cultural traits which emphasized educational and intellectual attainment, and argued that even though they were poor, Jewish and Asian Americans were middle class in outlook.[38]

William S. Egelman examined the educational experiences of Irish and Italian immigrants. He noted that the Irish immigrants brought with them a value system which gave high priority to educational achievement and that the Irish were quick to take advantage of the educational opportunities and have consistently shown higher educational achievement than the general population. He pointed out that the Italian immigrants had a different value system and they did not have great educational success. However, Egelman, through the use of NORC data, did indicate that in the 1980s Italian descendants were above national averages in educational achievement although still below the Irish Americans.[39]

Andrew Greeley, in agreement with Egelman, points out that in terms of education, income and occupational achievement, Irish Catholics are the most successful white gentile group in American society. He also argues that Irish Americans have maintained their cultural distinctiveness in their family life and their attitudes toward achievement.[40]

Malcolm W. Browne,[41] Robert B. Oxnam[42] and Stephen C. Graubard[43] stated that Asian Americans are more successful in the United States than many other groups because of their cultural values, such as, tightly knit families and their high respect for education which were brought over from their countries of origin in Asia. These authors argued that the attitudes, values and norms of Asian Americans which developed in their countries of origin are the key factors of their educational and occupational achievements in the United States.

Thomas Sowell, similarly, argued that the principal determinant of the economic success of an ethnic group in America consists of cultural traits its members brought over from the mother country. These cultural traits, according to Sowell, form the "human capital" of the group. That capital includes knowledge about making contacts, learning to use existing institutions, knowing how to find better jobs and how to get promoted. Sowell indicated that no trait in this cultural legacy is more important than the attitude of the ethnic group toward education. He stated that the subsequent high economic achievement of Jews and Asians in America is due to the respect for learning that these groups brought to America from their respective countries.[44]

In short, the researchers, cited and discussed above, assert that enduring cultural traits are the most important factors in explaining differences in behavior among the ethnic groups in the United States.

This author, after reviewing a substantial amount of the cultural trait approach literature, argues that major problems and weaknesses exist with this viewpoint in its understanding of the behavior of the different ethnic groups in America.

The first problem and weakness of the cultural trait approach is that cultural trait studies tend to contradict each other. For instance, some cultural trait studies say that the values of Italian immigrants hindered their children's success in the United States (for instance, Gambino[45]) while other cultural trait studies argue that the values of Italian immigrants promoted success for their children in this country (for instance, Briggs[46]). Continuing on this point, Egelman's study[47] on the Irish stated that traits brought over from Ireland promoted economic success for the Irish descendants in America while Thernstrom's work[48] stated that enduring cultural values hindered the economic success of Irish Americans in Boston. Based on the cultural trait research on the Irish and Italian Americans, it is not clear when cultural traits brought over from another country help or hinder a group.

Continuing on this discussion of contradictions within the cultural trait studies, Richard Gambino provided data within his own research that does not support his argument that Italian Americans have an enduring negative cultural attitude toward schooling. Richard Gambino found, in a 1969 survey of Americans, taken from the U.S. Bureau of the Census, the figure for Italian Americans in the age group between 25 and 34 completing high school was 50.4 percent and that this was the second highest percentage of all Americans in that age group. Gambino reported that in New York Italian Americans made up large percentages of the student body at SUNY, CUNY and the state's Catholic colleges. He noted that in the 1970s 34,000 out of the 169,000 students (or approximately 20 percent) at CUNY were Italian Americans, and indicated that Italian Americans accounted for 50 percent of Fordham University's student body.[49]

The second problem and weakness of the cultural trait approach is that the researchers of this approach do not examine the socioeconomic conditions that the different ethnic groups are living under in the United States (See Steinberg[50] and Lopreato[51]). The investigation of socioeconomic factors that an ethnic group is living under in America may provide more insight into why some ethnic groups succeed and others fail than simply a group's cultural traits (See Steinberg[52]). Researchers of the cultural trait approach, by examining only the cultural traits of a group and not the socioeconomic conditions that the group is living under in the United States, offer explanations for an ethnic group's success or lack of achievement that may not be based on a clear and complete understanding of all the facts. Works by Lopreato[53] and Steinberg[54] examined the socioeconomic conditions that ethnic groups' were living under and argued that cultural traits were less of a factor in influencing ethnic behavior than economic conditions.

Joseph Lopreato, in response to the cultural trait approach's allegations of a lack of achievement by Italian Americans', stated that there has been a tendency among those researchers to study Italian Americans in working class or poor areas. Lopreato noted that under these circumstances what observers have found may be relevant to Italian Americans of the lower and working classes; however, this may say little about Italian Americans in general. Italian American behavior, according to Lopreato, can be explained as more an outcome of socioeconomic differences rather than an outcome of differences in cultural traits.[55] Stephen Steinberg criticizes social science research that attributes ethnic inequality (poverty) to different value systems, and argues that ethnic and racial groups do differ in their aspirations and values but these cultural differences are the result of historical and economic factors. Steinberg asserts that the socioeconomic conditions that a group is living under create and maintain cultural values. He also argues that cultural values are not the primary factors in explaining behavioral characteristics.[56]

A third problem and weakness of the cultural trait approach is that it assumes that the economic structure of American society is totally open since this viewpoint argues that economic gains or failures of an ethnic group are based upon the group's norms attitudes and values and not what opportunities are available. However, this assumption is inaccurate. Melvin M. Tumin indicates that about 40 percent of the professionals in this country were sons and daughters of professionals. Tumin pointed out that this is nearly five times as many as would be expected in a perfectly open society. He argued that if a society was perfectly open, there would be no correlation between the occupation of a father and that of his sons or daughters, or between ascribed characteristics, and status.[57] Inheritance obviously plays an important role in determining an offspring's educational and occupational attainment in America. Furthermore, in examining intergenerational mobility, Peter M. Blau and Otis D. Duncan conclude that Americans as a whole are upwardly mobile, but that most individuals move only a step or two up the ladder.[58] Therefore, where an ethnic group starts from on the economic ladder (this is due to inheritance), plays an important role where the following generation will end up.[59]

The fourth problem and weakness of the cultural trait viewpoint is that the social scientists and writers who view cultural traits as independent variables base their research on speculation and impressions. For instance, the social scientists and writers of the cultural trait approach have no substantial evidence to show that the enduring cultural values and attitudes (brought over to America from a group's country of origin) promoted or hindered their economic achievement in this country. In other words, these researchers have no scientific data to support their claims about the successes or failures that result from an immigrant group's cultural traits. Works by Lopreato,[60] Grande,[61] and Broom and his associates[62] present data on the achievements of Italian Americans that do not provide support for the cultural trait approach's explanation for the Italian Americans supposed lack of achievement.

Joseph Lopreato pointed out that the "apparent low achievement" of Italian Americans as an outcome of a cultural trait brought over from Italy is inaccurate and misleading. Lopreato noted that the Italian peasants distrusted-and they still distrust-intellectuals for their constant abuses, not intellectualism or learning per se. He argued that early Italian immigrants did perceive, and correctly, that the school and teachers were hostile to the family. These immigrants, according to Lopreato, did not see the value of the education provided by the American high school because in school Italian children were advised to train for manual, working-class occupations and that many educators judged that they lacked the mental endowments necessary for other occupations. Moreover, Lopreato commented that the Italian families, sensing this, felt that the trades could be learned more readily and more expertly on the job while the youngster was being paid at the same time.[63]

Albert Grande stated that there were high percentages of Italian Americans in the learned professions and that this was proof that the Italian immigrant family did not have a negative attitude toward education. The Buffalo area, according to Grande, was an excellent example. Grande noted that there were large numbers of Italian-American physicians, lawyers, dentists and engineers, mostly from Buffalo's Sicilian West Side, and large numbers of Italian-Americans in highly responsible professional positions, i.e., presidents of medical and legal societies, heads of hospitals, judges and recipients of prestigious research grants. He pointed out that these accomplishments could not have come so soon from a cultural trait (brought over from Italy to the United States) hostile to education and intellectual attainment.[64]

J. Lopreato in *Italian Americans*[65] discussed a study conducted by Leonard Broom and his associates. Leonard Broom and his associates calculated indicators of rank for education, income and occupations and compared various racial and ethnic groups on that basis. The native-whites were taken as the norm or point of reference. Key findings of Broom's study showed that the highest achievement had been exhibited by the Russians, Greeks and Italians (in that order) while the representatives of the old immigration (Anglo-Canadians, Germans, French-Canadians and Irish) rank in achievement either below the native norm-white (the point of reference) or slightly above it. Specifically, with respect to the second-generation Italians, this study showed that they are at about the norm in educational attainment, slightly higher in occupation and much higher in income.[66]

There is also a lack of evidence to show that enduring cultural values promoted a supposed economic success for Jews in the United States. For instance, works by Wolfe,[67] and Schappes[68] do not provide support for the cultural trait studies on Jewish Americans.

Anna C. Wolfe estimated that of the nation's six million Jews, between 700,000 and 800,000 are poor. These large numbers suggest that being steeped in Jewish culture by no means guaranteed delivery from poverty.[69]

In a review, Morris Schappes pointed out that the concentration of Jews in the professions and certain white collar occupations tends to obscure the fact that a large number of Jews are still working class.[70] In the 1970s about 30 percent of adult Jewish males were employed outside business and the professions.[71]

The fifth problem and weakness of the cultural trait approach is that these researchers tend to view cultural traits as stagnant in nature. For instance, by stating that one's cultural traits inhibit a group from advancing economically suggests that cultural traits are stagnant and unchanging. In contrast to this belief, Edward Shils argued that traditions (cultural traits) are always evolving, changing, can synthesize with other cultural traits and are able to adapt to the changing environment. Moreover, Shils pointed out that if a cultural trait (tradition) cannot adapt to a changing environment (this would include changing economic opportunities) it will be replaced or modified.[72] In other words, cultural traits alone do not inhibit economic mobility or progress.[73]

Richard Alba's work exemplified Shils' argument about cultural traits. He pointed out that Italian-Americans (and for that matter, other white ethnic groups) are becoming similar to majority Americans in the important matters of social standing as well as those of culture. Although the author noted that ethnic values (traits) pertaining to Italian Americans have not altogether disappeared, his data indicated that these cultural values brought over from Italy did not constitute a barrier to the educational and occupational achievements of the Italian Americans of the 1980s. Furthermore, Alba indicated that these values are not serious impediments to social relations, such as intermarriage. Alba listed the significant changes which have occurred among Italian Americans over the past century. These changes included the loss of the Italian language by the third generation, the shrinkage of Italian immigrant communities, a considerable economic and occupational mobility of this group over the past decades, the erosion of past cultural traits, and the Italian Americans' increasing rates of intermarriage with other ethnic and religious groups. Thus, Alba demonstrated that ethnic values associated with Italian Americans were disappearing and that this disappearance was an outcome of socioeconomic conditions which exist in the United States, (that is, cultural traits being replaced or modified as an outcome of a changing environment).[74]

Finally, the most serious problem and weakness of the cultural trait approach is that it does not examine the historical migration patterns of the different immigrant groups (that is, the time period and the permanency of migration, and the educational and occupational background of the ethnic group before migration). In examining the historical migration patterns, one can see why some groups would become more successful than others in the United States.

J. Lopreato noted that, over the years, there has been a tendency by scholars to compare Italian Americans to more successful ethnic groups (i.e., Jewish Americans and Irish Americans) and then suggest that Italians are low and poor achievers.[75] Albert Grande argued that there was little basis for a comparative study of occupational achievement in the United States between Southern Italians and Jews, for example. Grande pointed out that Southern Italian immigrants had the highest rate of illiteracy among the European ethnic groups which emigrated during the turn of the twentieth century while the Jewish immigrants from Eastern Europe were educationally diverse. He noted that most of these Jewish immigrants could read and write Yiddish and knew enough Hebrew to read prayers. In other words, the advantage that Jews had upon their arrival in America in terms of urban skills (education) was great in comparison to the Italians. The upward climb of the Jews had been more rapid because Jewish immigrants came from different levels of European society including the commercial, professional and educated classes-- while the Italian mass immigration was made up predominantly of poorly educated people from the lowest economic level.[76]

Stephen Steinberg, in a similar discussion, indicated that in spite of their poverty the early Jewish immigrants (that is, in 1899 to 1910) were concentrated in economically advanced parts of their countries of origin, and they had experiences and occupational skills that would serve them quite well in the expanding industrial economy of the United States. In contrast, he stated that the vast majority of Italians who came to America during the same period were farmers or farmhands (mostly unskilled laborers). Steinberg noted that among the early Jewish immigrants two thirds or 67 percent of the adult labor force were skilled laborers, while only 15 percent of the adult labor force of the Southern Italian immigrants was skilled. The economically upward climb of Jewish Americans had been more rapid than the Italian-Americans because they came to the United States at a higher rung of the economic ladder. It is important to note that Italians and Jews are constantly being compared (possibly because they emigrated to the United States at about the same time and were two of the largest groups of immigrants), and the results of these comparisons have been mistakenly used to draw conclusions about the Italians.[77]

Continuing on this migration pattern examination, differences in levels of achievement between the Italian and Irish-Americans can at least partly be explained by the differences in migration patterns (that is, time and permanency of migration). Over 60 percent of the Irish immigrants came to the United States between the years of 1820 and 1900[78] while 60 percent of the Italian immigrants arrived in this country between 1900 and 1914.[79] One can see that the Irish in general came to America one, two and even three generations before the Italians and thus would have had a significant head start in socioeconomic advancement over the Italians. Furthermore, when the Irish migrated to the United States, they came with their families and intended to stay in America.[80] The Italian immigrants, on the other hand, were mostly men and many returned to Italy. Few Italian families from 1900 to 1914 were coming to America.[81] Rodney Stark pointed out that a great many Italians with family stayed in America because of the outbreak of World War I and the bad conditions that existed in Italy after the War. They decided to wait for a later time to return to their country of origin. However, Stark noted that many Italians never did go back and he argued as long as the Italians thought they would return, they were likely to maintain Italian cultural values. This would include a mistrust of educators and educational institutions outside the family. He did indicate that, as time passed, the maintenance of Italian cultural values and norms by the immigrants began to disappear and the Italians began to participate more fully in American society.[82]

In comparing the occupations of immigrants before their arrival to the United States, Steinberg indicated that a major segment of Asian immigration represented educational and occupational elite. He showed that from 1965 to 1977 almost 50 percent of all Asian immigrants were professionals before coming to the United States while only 25 percent of other immigrant groups from the same time period who came to America were professionals. In other words, many Asians were already successful before their arrival to the United States in comparison to other groups. Furthermore, Steinberg noted that it is not valid to compare the children of upper middle class Asian professionals to the children of working class or poor groups as is done when Asians are compared to other ethnic groups.[83]

Overall, the studies of the cultural trait approach contain contradictions, do not examine the socioeconomic conditions that the groups were living under in the United States, assume that the American economic structure is totally open to all its members, and are based on impressions and speculations and not based on substantial data and evidence. These studies also tend to view cultural traits as stagnant. Finally, and most importantly, the cultural trait studies fail to examine the historical migration patterns of a group.

This author argues that it has been too common for many researchers to take for granted that the behavior of an ethnic group is primarily based on enduring cultural traits. The cultural trait approach alone does not provide an adequate explanation of the behavior of ethnic groups in America (or in any other country). An immigrant group's cultural traits are not the primary element in explaining a group's economic successes or failures in the United States.

More statistical studies need to investigate the following conditions in order to understand the different rates of mobility and successes experienced by the various American immigrant groups: 1) the time period of the ethnic group's migration, the area of the United States where the group settled, and the permanency of the migration; 2) the resources that each ethnic group brought with them when they came to a particular section of the United States (that is, the educational and occupational background of the group before their migration to the United States); and 3) the economic opportunities that were available to the various immigrant groups within the different areas of the United States and during the different time periods of American history.[84] By investigating these socioeconomic factors, one can determine how attitudes and values are developed and maintained within certain immigrant groups, since the attitudes and values that human beings create and maintain always arise within specific environmental circumstances.[85]

NOTES

1. Originally published by the John D. Calandra Institute, Topical Issues Series at City University of New York, New York, NY, 2001.
2. Sowell, Thomas, *Ethnic America: A History,* New York, NY: Basic Books, 1981.
3. Ibid.
4. Kroeber, Alfred, *Anthropology,* New York, NY: Harcourt Jovanovich, 1948.
5. Kroeber, Alfred and Parsons, Talcott, "The Concept of Culture and of Social Systems," *American Sociological Review,* 23, 1958.
6. Parsons, Talcott, *The Social System,* Glencoe, IL: The Free Press, 1951, "Sociological Theory," *Encyclopedia Britannica 20,* 1967 and "On Building Social System Theory, A Personal History," *Daedalus 9,* 1970.

7. Strodtbeck, Fred, "Family Interaction, Values and Achievement" in Sklare, M. (editor), *The Jews: Social Patterns of an American Group,* New York, NY: The Free Press, 1958.

8. Rosen, Bernard C., "Race, Ethnicity and the Achievement Syndrome," *American Sociological Review* 24, 1959.

9. Gordon, Milton M., *Assimilation in American Life,* New York, NY: Oxford University Press, 1964.

10. Covello, Leonard, *The Sociological Background of the Italo American School Child,* Leiden, Netherlands: E. J. Brill, 1967.

11. Glazer, Nathan and Moynihan, Daniel P., *Beyond the Melting Pot,* Cambridge,MA: The M. I. T. Press, 1971.

12. Thernstrom, Stephen, *The Other Bostonians: Poverty and Progress in the American Metropolis, 1880–1970,* Cambridge, MA: Harvard University Press, 1972.

13. Greeley Andrew, and McCready, William C., "The Transmission of Cultural Heritage: The Case of the Irish and the Italians" in N. Glazer and D. P, NY. Moynihan (editors), *Ethnicity,* Cambridge, MA: Harvard University Press, 1975.

14. Gambino, Richard, *Blood of My Blood,* Garden City, NY: Doubleday and Company, 1974.

15. LaGumina, Salvatore and Cavaioli, Frank, *The Ethnic Dimension in American Society,* Boston, MA: Holbrook Press, 1974.

16. Kessner, Thomas, *The Golden Door,* New York, NY: Oxford University, 1977.

17. Briggs, John Walker, *An Italian Passage: Immigrants to Three American cities, 1870–1930,* New Haven, CT: Yale University, 1978.

18. Greeley, Andrew M., *The Irish Americans: The Rise to Money and Power,* New York, NY: Harper and Row, 1981 and *The Catholic Myth: The Behavior and Beliefs of American Catholics,* New York, NY: MacMillan Publishers Company, 1990.

19. Glazer, Nathan, *Ethnic Dilemmas, 1964–1982,* Cambridge, MA: Harvard University Press, 1983, *The New Immigration: A Challenge to American Society,* San Diego, CA: San Diego State University Press, 1988 and *The Limits of Social Policy,* Cambridge, MA: Harvard University Press, 1988.

20. Egelman, William, "Italian and Irish Americans in Education: A Sociohistoric Analysis" in Feminella, Francis X. (editor), *Italians and Irish in America,* Staten Island: American Historical Association, 1985.

21. Browne, Malcolm W., "A Look at Young Asians," *New York Times,* March 25, 1986.

22. Oxnam, Robert B., "Why Asians Succeed Here," *New York Times Magazine,* November 20, 1986.

23. Graubard, Stephen G., "Why Do Asian Pupils Win These Prizes?" *New York Times,* January 19, 1988.

24. Sowell, Thomas, *Ethnic America: A History,* New York, NY: Basic Books, 1981, *Is Reality Optional?* Paolo Alto, CA: Hoover Institute Press, 1993, and *Migration and Cultures: A World View,* New York, NY: Basic Books, 1996.

25. Strodtbeck, "Family Interaction, Values and Achievement," 1958.

26. Rosen, "Race, Ethnicity and the Achievement Syndrome," 1959.

27. Gordon, *Assimilation in American Life,* 1964: 185–187.

28. Covello, *The Sociological Background of the Italo American School Child,* 1967.

29. Glazer and Moynihan, *Beyond the Melting Pot,* 1971.

30. Thernstrom, *The Other Bostonians: Poverty and Progress in the American Metropolis, 1880–1970*, 1973.

31. Gambino, *Blood of My Blood*, 1974.

32. LaGumina and Cavaioli, *The Ethnic Dimension in America Society*, 1974:339.

33. Greeley and McCready, "The Case of the Irish and the Italians," 1975:229–30.

34. Kessner, *The Golden Door*, 1977.

35. Briggs, *An Italian Passage: Immigrants to Three American Cities, 1870–1930*, 1978.

36. See Glazer, *Ethnic Dilemmas, 1964–1982*, 1983, *The New Immigration: A Challenge to American Society*, 1988, and *The Limits of Social Policy*, 1988.

37. Glazer, *Ethnic Dilemmas, 1964–1982*, 1983:61.

38. See Glazer, *Ethnic Dilemmas, 1964–1982*, 1983, *The New Immigration: A Challenge to American Society*, 1988, and *The Limits of Social Policy*, 1988.

39. Egelman, "Italians and Irish Americans in Education: A Sociohistoric Analysis," 1985.

40. Greeley, *The Irish Americans: The Rise to Money and Power*, 1981 and *The Catholic Myth: The Behavior and Beliefs of American Catholics*, 1990.

41. Browne, "A Look at Young Asians," 1986.

42. Oxnam, "Why Asians Succeed Here?" 1986.

43. Graubard, "Why Do Asian Pupils Win These Prices?" 1988.

44. Sowell, *Ethnic America: A History*, 1981.

45. Gambino, *Blood of My Blood*, 1974.

46. Briggs, *An Italian Passage: Immigrants to Three American Cities, 1870–1930*, 1978.

47. Egelman, "Italian and Irish Americans in Education: A Sociohistoric Analysis," 1985.

48. Thernstrom, *The Other Bostonians: Poverty and Progress in the Americans Metropolis, 1880–1970*, 1973.

49. Gambino, *Blood of My Blood*, 1974: 246–266,

50. Steinberg, Stephen, *The Ethnic Myth*, Boston, MA: Beacon Press, 1989 and *Turning Back: The Retreat from Racial Justice: Am American Thought*, Boston, MA: Beacon Press, *1995.*

51. Lopreato, Joseph, *Italian Americans*, New York, NY: Random House, 1970.

52. Steinberg, *The Ethnic Myth*, 1989 and *Turning Back: The Retreat from Racial Justice: American Thought, 1995.*

53. Loreato, *Italian Americans*, 1970.

54. Steinberg, *Turning Back: The Retreat from Racial Justice: An American Thought*, 1995.

55. Lopreato, *Italian Americans*, 1970.

56. Steinberg, *The Ethnic Myth, 1989* and *Turning Back: The Retreat from Racial Justice: An American Thought, 1995.*

57. Tumin, Melvin E., *Patterns of Society*, Boston, MA: Little Brown, 1973.

58. . Blau, Peter M. and Duncan, Otis, *The American Occupation Structure*, New York, NY: Wiley, 1967.

59. Steinberg, *The Ethnic Myth,* 1989.

60. Lopreato, Italian *Americans*, 1970.

61. Grande, Albert, "The Intellectual Image of Italian Americans," *Unico Magazine*, Vol. 35, No. 5, 1980.

62. Broom, Leonard, Martin, Cora Ann and Maynard, Betty, "Status Profile of Racial and Ethnic Populations" (paper read at the meetings of the Pacific Sociological Association, Long Beach CA, March 1967), also discussed in Lopreato, *Italian Americans,* 1970.

63. Lopreato, *Italian Americans,* 1970:154.

64. Grande, "The Intellectual Image of Italian Americans," 1980: 12–13.

65. Lopreato, *Italian Americans,* 1970.

66. Broom and his associates, "Status Profiles of Racial and Ethnic Populations, 1967, also discussed in Lopreato, *Italian Americans,* 1970.

67. Wolfe, Anna C., "The Invisible Jewish Poor" in Levine, N. and Hochbaum, M. (editors), *Poor Jews,* New Brunswick, NJ: Transactions Books, 1974.

68. Schappes, Morris, "Review of Nathan Glazer's American Judaism," *Journal of Ethnic Studies,* Fall 1973.

69. Wolfe, "The Invisible Jewish Poor, 1974:36.

70. Schappes, "Review of Glazer's American Judaism,"1973:98.

71. Steinberg, *The Ethnic Myth,* 1989.

72. Shils, Edward, *Tradition,* Chicago, IL: The University of Chicago Press, 1981.

73. Alba, Richard, *Italian Americans into the Twilight of Ethnicity,* Englewood Cliffs, New Jersey: Prentice–Hall, 1985.

74. Ibid.

75. Lopreato, *Italian Americans,* 1970.

76. Grande, Albert, The Cultural and Intellectual Experience of Italian–Americans: Some Observations," in Nelli, Humbert, *The United States and Italy: The First Two Hundred Years,* Staten Island, NY: American Italian Historical Association, 1977.

77. Stenberg, *Ethnic Myth,* 1989.

78. Stone, Frank, *The Irish of Connecticut,* Storrs, CT: Ethnic Heritage Series, 1975: 22.

79. Alba, *Italian Americans into the Twilight of Ethnicity,* 1985:45.

80. Stone, *The Irish of Connecticut,* 1975.

81. Rodney Stark, *Sociology,* Belmont, CA: Wadsworth Publishing Co., 1985:44.

82. Ibid.

83. Steinberg, *The Ethnic Myth,* 1989:274.

84. See Healey, J., *Race, Ethnicity and Gender in the United States: Inequality, Group Conflict and Power,* Thousand Oaks, CA: Pine Forge Press, 1997, Gesualdi, Louis, *The Italian Immigrants of Connecticut, 1880–1940,* New Haven, Connecticut: Connecticut Academy of Arts and Sciences, 1997, Steinberg, *The Ethnic Myth,* 1989 and Steinberg, *Turning Back: The Retreat from Racial Justice: An American Thought and Policy,* 1995.

85. Ibid.

CHAPTER 5

POPULARLY HELD BELIEFS ABOUT ITALIAN AMERICANS AND ORGANIZED CRIME[1]

As we are now in the middle of the first decade of the twenty-first century, there still exist disturbing and popularly held beliefs about Italian Americans and organized crime in the United States. This chapter examines the popularly held beliefs about Italian Americans and organized crime by briefly reviewing studies indicating that this ethnic group continues to be negatively portrayed on television and in the movies and that a high percentage of Americans still has a disapproving perception of this group. Secondly, this chapter presents data that do not support these negative beliefs and makes some recommendations to deal with the negative depictions and mistaken understanding of Italian Americans. Let us look at some recent studies showing negative beliefs about Italian Americans held in the United States.

The results of S. Robert Lichter and Daniel R. Amundon's report Portrayal of Italian American Characters in Prime Television Series 1994-1995 show that Italian Americans are rarely seen as heroes or ever in a high status role on television. The study found evidence of popular culture's continuing association of Italian Americans with organized crime.[2]

Bill Dal Cerro's research Italian Culture on Film 1928-1999 analyzes the portraying of Italian/American in movies over a 70-year period. Results of the research reveal a consistent negative portrayal of Italian/Americans (that is 74 percent of the films involving Italian/Americans). Of all the movies dealing with Italian/Americans, images of Italian/Americans as violent criminals predominates (41 percent), followed by portrayals of boors, buffoons, bigots and other social undesirables (33 percent). These figures clearly indicate an entrenched, institutionalized bias against Americans of Italian descent in the entertainment industry.[3]

The National Public Opinion Research for Commission for Social Justice Order Sons of Italy in America's study Americans of Italian Descent: A Study of Public Images, Beliefs and Misperceptions[4] reports that 74 percent of the U.S. public sees Italian Americans associated with organized crime. Richard A. Capozzola's work *Finalmente: The Truth about Organized Crime*[5] suggests that the media and politicians, by exaggerating the role of Italian Americans in organized crime, have influenced the public's inaccurate and negative perception of this ethnic group. This exaggeration includes that Italian Americans developed organized crime in the United States and that a significant percentage of Italian Americans are involved in the Mafia.

Zogby International's National Survey: American Teenagers and Stereotyping reveals that teens learn the less admirable aspects of their heritage from entertainment industry stereotyping. The Report indicates that 46percent of Italian American teens said that television's portrayal of Italian Americans as crime bosses is accurate and 30 percent said that they were proud of their TV image. Moreover, the Report shows that 78 percent of all American teenagers associate Italian Americans with criminal activities.[6] It needs to be added that a Princeton study revealed 74 percent of Americans feel all Italian Americans are connected to the mob.

Overall, these recent studies indicate that Italian Americans are still portrayed and perceived as being involved in criminality and socially undesirable behavior. Moreover, these studies show that many Americans believe Italian Americans developed organized crime in the United States and a significant percentage of Italian Americans are involved in the Mafia. However, social scientific studies do not support these commonly held beliefs about Italian Americans. This article will now present data that do not support these commonly held beliefs.[7]

Research points out that Italian Americans did not develop organized crime in the United States. First, H. Abadinsky's book Organized Crime points out that organized crime existed in the United States before the arrival of the large numbers of Italian immigrants from 1880 to 1920. This study discusses the practices by such famous nineteenth century businessmen as John Jacob Astor, Cornelius Vanderbilt, John D. Rockefeller, and others. Such practices included extortion, blackmail, violence, bribery, murder and the use of thugs and private armies to destroy a competitor. This work verifies that the practices of the nineteenth century businessmen were no different from the practices of Italian American gangsters of the 20th century. Moreover, the book indicates that the social, economic, historical and cultural conditions in the United States produced organized crime.[8]

Second, D. Cauchon's article "Head of BCCI-linked Bank Quits,"[9] A. Block and F. Scarpitti's book *Poisoning for Profit: The Mafia and Toxic Waste*[10] and W. Chambliss' study *On the Take: From Petty Crooks to Presidents*[11] detail the huge involvement of the police, big businesses, and the CIA in the development of organized crime groups. In addition, J. Mills' book The *Underground Empire: Where Crime and Government Embrace* presents evidence revealing that the United States government has been a major player in international drug crime systems.[12] These works show the role that the government (including the CIA and the police) and big business have played in the growth of organized crime in the U.S.

Third, V. Kappeler, M. Blumberg, and G. Potter's book *The Mythology of Crime and Criminal Justice* describes the prevalent practices employed by the media, law enforcement personnel, and government officials to manipulate information and create crime myths. Some of these practices involve creating criminal stereotypes, interjecting personal opinion into media presentation without factual basis; presenting certain facts and not others; and presenting supposedly factual information with undocumented sources of authority. Their work indicates that the media, law enforcement personnel and government officials have used such practices to blame Italian Americans for developing organized crime. Furthermore, their book convincingly argues that the socioeconomic conditions of American society need to be investigated in order to understand the cause of organized crime.[13]

Data indicate that contrary to popular belief a significant percentage of Italian Americans are not involved in the Mafia. As a matter of fact, only a fraction of 1 percent of all Italian Americans participates in organized crime.[14]

According to the Federal Bureau of Investigation, there were allegedly 5,000 Italian American who were made members of the Mafia at the height of involvement. Currently there are supposedly 1,500 Italian Americans who are members of the Mafia out of 20 million Italian Americans. Furthermore, of an estimated 500,000 members of organized crime in America today, Italian Americans make up a slim 0.3 percent of all involved.[15]

In short, the evidence demonstrates that the widely held beliefs about Italian Americans and organized crime are not true. The data show that Italian Americans did not develop organized crime in the United States and only a fraction of a percentage of all Italian Americans participates in organized crime. What's more, social scientific research points out social, economic, historical and cultural factors of American society gave rise to organized crime.

The reasons, according to this author, for blaming Italian Americans for organized crime are as follows. First, the media finds Italian American organized crime stories profitable. Second, some politicians, especially when their opponent is Italian American, find associating Italian Americans with organized crime useful for winning votes.

It is this author's opinion that as long as the above and widely held belief about Italian Americans and organized crime continues to exist in the United States, organized crime will not be dealt with properly. Kappeler, Blumberg, and Potter's *The Mythology of Crime and Criminal Justice* indicates that the media, law enforcement personnel and the U.S. government need to be held accountable for the blaming of a single ethnic group for the development of organized crime in the United States.[16] Moreover, law enforcement agencies, big businesses and the government need to take responsibility for their part in participating in many organized activities. For instance, David R. Simon's book Elite Deviance examines the institutionalized set of deviant practices by elites (persons form the highest strata of U.S. society) that are international. His book points out these elites' collaboration with organized crime involved in the 850 billion dollars global narcotics trade and the vast amount of money laundered by legitimate financial institutions, lawyers and other elite professionals.[17]

To deal with organized crime more successfully according to this author, it makes sense to think of organized crime as a business that provides illegal goods and services, rather than an Italian or alien conspiracy. It needs to be recognized that organized crime is able to flourish primarily because of the high demand for goods and services (for instance, drugs) that have been designated as illegal.

Moreover, efforts need to focus on identifying and dealing with political, corporate and financial deviance that serves as links between the underworld and upper world. For example, Stephen M. Rossoff, Henry W. Pontell and Robert Tillman's book *Profit without Honor: White Collar Crime and the Looting of America* points out that corrupt banks are central to the operations of organized crime that import billions of dollars of illegal drugs into the U.S.[18]

In conclusion, recent studies indicate that Italian Americans are inaccurately portrayed and misperceived as being involved in criminality and socially undesirable behavior. Moreover, research shows organized crime is able to flourish primarily because of the high demand for goods and services that have been designated as illegal and not because it is an Italian or alien conspiracy.

Finally, this chapter makes the following recommendations, based on R. A. Capozzola's *Finalmente: The Truth about Organized Crime*[19] and Carol Chiago Lujinnos' study "The Only Real Indian is the Stereotyped Indian,"[20] to deal with the incorrect, negative representations and misunderstanding of Italian Americans, previously stated. First, more Italian Americans need to support and participate in such organizations as the Order Sons of Italy in America, the National Italian American Foundation and Unico National. Second, more Italian Americans need to voice their protests, concerns, or objections by phoning or writing to radio stations, television networks, newspapers, magazines that offend their group as well as other groups. Third, more Italian Americans need to hold accountable politicians, actors, celebrities, and writers who assist in portraying Italian Americans, as well as other groups, falsely and negatively. Fourth, more Italian Americans need to boycott movies, TV shows, products and businesses that offend their group as well as other groups. Fifth, more Italian Americans need to speak up when someone is saying something that is inaccurate and offensive about their group and about other groups. Sixth, long-term efforts to reduce negative stereotyping of Italian Americans include establishing and supporting Italian American studies programs at both state and privately funded educational institutions. Seventh, books and other publications in law, government, history, and the social sciences need to include a more widespread analysis of the Italian American experience. Eighth, Italian Americans need to become more noticeable and concerned in politics, law and education, as well as other leadership ranks, to support more truthful representation of Italian Americans.

NOTES

1. Originally unpublished paper, 2006.

2. Lichter S. Robert and Amundon, Daniel R.*Portrayal of Italian American Character in Prime Television Series, 1994–1995,* Washington, D.C.: Social Justice Order Sons of Italy in America, 1996.

3. Dal Cerro, Bill, *Italian Culture on Film, 1928–1999,* Floral Park, NY: Italic Studies Institute Image Research Project, 1999.

4. *Americans of Italian Decent: A Study of Public Images, Beliefs and Misperceptions,* Washington, D.C.: The National Public Opinion Research for Commission for Social Justice Order Sons of Italy, 1991.

5. Capozzola, Richard A., Finalmente: The Truth about Organized Crime, Altamonte Springs, FL: Five Centuries Books, 2001.

6. Zogby International Survey: American Teenagers and Stereotyping, Utica, NY: Zogby International, 2001.

7. Alfano, M., "Negative Stereotype Persist through FBI Figures Reveal Facts," ComUnico Magazine, April 2002.

8. Abadinsky, Howard, *Organized Crime,* Chicago, IL: Nelson Hall, 1985.

9. Cauchon, D., "Head of BCCI–Link Bank Quits," *USA Today,* August 15, 1991.

10. Block, A., and Scarpitti, F., *Poisoning for Profit: The Mafia and Toxic Waste,* New York, NY: William Morrow, 1985.

11. Chambliss, William, *On the Take: From Petty Crooks to Presidents,* Bloomington, IN: Indiana University Press, 1978.

12. Mills, J., The Underground Empire: Where Crime and Government and Embrace, New York, NY: Doubleday, 1986.

13. Kappeler, V., Blumberg, M. and Potter, G., *The Mythology of Crime and Criminal Justice,* Prospect Heights, Illinois: Waveland Press, 2000.

14. Gambino, Richard,"America's Most Tolerated Intolerance: Bigotry against Italian Americans," *The Italian American Review,* Spring/Summer, 1997.

15. Alfano, "Negative Stereotypes Persist though FBI Figures Reveal Facts," April 2002.

16. Kappeler, Blumberg and Potter, The Mythology of Crime and Criminal Justice, 2000.

17. Simon's, David R., *Elite Deviance,* Boston, MA: Allyn and Bacon, 1999.

18. Rossoff, Stephen M., Pontell, Henry W. and Tillman, Robert *Profit without Honor: White Collar Crime and the Looting of America,* Upper Saddle River, NJ: Pearson Education, Inc., 2002.

19. Capozzola, Finalmente: The Truth about Organized Crime, 1994.

20. Lujinnos, Carol Chiago, "The Only Real Indian is the Stereotyped Indian" in Mann, Caramae Rickey and. Zatz, Marjorie S (editors), *Images of Color Images of Crime,* Los Angeles, CA: Roxbury Publishing Co., 1998.

CHAPTER 6

BRUHN AND WOLF'S STUDY OF ROSETO, PENNSYLVANIA: A BRIEF DISCUSSION[1]

This chapter discusses John G. Bruhn and Stewart Wolf's *The Roseto Story: An Anatomy of Health*. Bruhn and Wolf's study (sixteen years of research beginning in the early 1960s) investigates the Italian community of Roseto, Pennsylvania. The book's findings indicate that a close knit community (such as the Italian-American community of Roseto) acts as an area of defense against the effects of stress, bereavement and life changes.[2]

The Roseto Story demonstrates that the traditional community life established in Italy was continued by first and second generation Italian-Americans in Roseto, Pennsylvania. Bruhn and Wolf's study describes how the extended family and social organizations (such as mutual benefit societies, religious organizations and others) kept Roseto a closely knit Italian-American community. The book makes evident that the extended families of Roseto's Italian-Americans provided assistance for their members (that is, caring for sick and elderly members). Moreover, the text points out that the social organizations provided support for the cohesiveness among Italian-Americans in Roseto.[3]

Bruhn and Wolf found that the Italian- American community support systems of Roseto, PA appear to be a major factor in Roseto's lower rate of fatal heart attacks. They indicate that from 1955 to 1961, the death from heart attacks in Roseto was less than one third the average in the United States. The authors explain that traditional community life played a key role in the low rate of heart attacks among these Italian-Americans.

Bruhn and Wolf's book shows that younger, college educated Italian-Americans (third generation) from Roseto found Roseto's traditional rules and values of the extended family and social organizations to be unsuitable with social mobility and career promotion. The text points out that these college edu-cated Italian-Americans adopted a lifestyle typical of middle-class Americans (that is more individual oriented than group oriented) and became heart attack victims. Furthermore, the text indicates that by the early 1970s, the previously traditional community life was almost non-existent among the grandchildren of the original Italian-Americans of Roseto, and that fatal heart attacks began to occur among young third generation Italian-American men of Roseto for the first time.[4]

The Roseto Story determines that when a close knit community (such as Ro-seto) no longer provided solid social support, heart attacks among these Italian-Americans increased. Traditional community life had been of great benefit to the physical and mental health of the people of Roseto. In conclusion, Bruhn and Wolf demonstrate the importance of community bonds to good health.[5]

NOTES

1. Originally published in *ComUnico Magazine,* October 2000.

2. Bruhn, John G. and Wolf, Stewart, *The Roseto Story: An Anatomy of Health,* Norman, OK: University of Oklahoma Press, 1979.

3. Ibid.

4. Ibid.

5. Ibid.

CHAPTER 7

GIOVANNI SCHIAVO'S WORKS: A SUMMARY[1]

Giovanni Schiavo, according to many academics, was a remarkable American historian. Although he was practically unknown to the general public, Schiavo was well respected for his writings by many American scholars. Before his death at age eighty-five in 1983, Schiavo had devoted and dedicated sixty years of his life to researching and publishing works on the Italian American experience. He left American society, a rich legacy in his books. It is this author's hope that more people will become aware of Schiavo's research and interested in reading his books. This essay sums up Schiavo's key studies.

First, Giovanni Schiavo, in *The Italians in America before the Civil War*, wrote about the Italian Americans who had helped build the United States before the Civil War. He described the Italian influence of American culture and presented an impressive list of Italian navigators and pioneers in the United States.[2]

Second, Schiavo's book, *Italian American History, Vol. I*, is a historical study on Italian music and musicians in America. This work also provides an account of the Italian-Americans who held public office in the United States from the 1700s to the 1940s.[3]

Third, Giovanni Schiavo, in *Italian American History, Vol. II*, discussed the Italian contribution to the Catholic Church in America. He listed the brave actions of Italian religious men and women in the United States, and also presented a history of the Italian parishes in America[4]

Fourth, Schiavo's work, *Four Centuries of Italian-American History*, prepared a historical outline of the Italians in America. It traces Italians in America from Columbus to the end of World War II.[5]

Fifth, Giovanni Schiavo, in *The Truth about the Mafia and Organized Crime*, dispelled the many myths about Italians and crime. He showed that organized crime in America did not originate with the Italian immigrants. Moreover, Schiavo successfully demonstrated that Italians never had a major control of organized crime in the United States.[6]

Finally, Schiavo's text, *The Italians in America before the Revolution*, detailed the Italian American contribution in the economic, commercial, political and cultural activities before the American Revolution. This book contains twenty chapters on the contributions made to America by such Italians as Christopher Columbus, Amerigo Vespucci, John Cabot, Giovanni Da Verrazzano, Marcos De Niza, Enrico Tonti, Alphonse Tonti, Father Bressani, Father Chino, William Paca, Philip Mazzei, Francis Vigo, Carlo Bellini, Onorio Razzolini, Giuseppe Ceracchi, James Philip Puglia, Giovanni Battista Saratori and Paolo Busti[7].

In conclusion, it is important for an ethnic group to be cognizant of their ethnic heritage and to take what is deemed productive and useful to creating their lives. However, it is also important to be people who in knowing about their own ethnic group's history will also have a comprehension of the lives of other groups. All groups need to be seen in their own contexts of time and place in history. The reading of Giovanni Schiavo's books is a meaningful beginning to an understanding of the ethnic group experience in the United States.

NOTES

1. Originally published in *ComUnico Magazine*, October 2000.

2. Schiavo, Giovanni, *The Italians in America before the Civil War*, New York, NY: The Vigo Press, 1934.

3. Schiavo, Giovanni, *Italian American History, Vol. I*, New York, NY: The Vigo Press, 1947.

4. Schiavo, Giovanni, *Italian American History, Vol. II*, New York, NY: The Vigo Press, 1949.

5. Schiavo, Giovanni, *Four Centuries of Italian–American History, 5 editions*, New York, NY: The Vigo Press, 1952–58.

6. Schiavo, Giovanni, *The Truth about the Mafia and Organized Crime*, New York, NY: The Vigo Press, 1952.

7. Schiavo, Giovanni, *The Italians in America before the Revolution*, New York, NY and Dallas, TX: The Vigo Press, 1976.

CHAPTER 8

PRAISES FOR GIOVANNI SCHIAVO[1]

Giovanni Schiavo was considered the father of Italian American studies. Many scholars and writers have highly praised Schiavo's contribution to ethnic studies. The purpose of this chapter, as a continuation of the previous chapter "Giovanni Schiavo's Works: A Summary," is to document such praises. The information for this article was drawn from the Schiavo collection located in the Research Library of the American-Italian Renaissance Foundation (New Orleans, Louisiana).[2]

Peter Sammartino in the *Italian-American Digest* stated:

> Giovanni Schiavo was a combination of a historian and investigative reporter. The extent of his research was formidable. While there had been persons before him who might have delved into the history of either person, a place or an event, Schiavo covered everything. No one has approached him in the sheer quality of his investigations into the role of Italians in America, in the United States or anywhere in the world....Scores of academic people fed on his findings for generations. Whatever we Americans of Italian heritage lay claim to in the history of our country, was due mainly to his research.[3]

Philip di Franco in *The Italian American Experience* wrote the following about Schiavo.

> Giovanni Schiavo was, unquestionably, the most diligent, devoted and dedicated writer, researcher, historian and publisher of the Italian American world. The man was truly remarkable for his tireless efforts in acquiring and disseminating knowledge and information on the Italian experience in America. Everyone who has written about the Italian American finds him or herself swallowed by his awesome sources of information. We have all benefited from the

toil of this man, and in his lifetime he was not properly recognized for his superb achievement. *Tante grazie*, Giovanni[4].

Philip J. DiNovo in "Giovanni Schiavo, Author and Historian" said:

> Giovanni Schiavo dedicated his lifetime to research and documentation of the contributions made by Italian Americans to the United States at a tremendous cost....Historian Schiavo was the first to inform us of the significant role Italians have played in American history. We owe him a great debt; it is too bad that he didn't receive the gratitude and honors from the Italian American community he deserved.[5]

Anthony Sorrentino in *Organizing the Ethnic Community* expressed the following.

> He was truly a pioneer in ethnic studies, and over the years he wrote almost a dozen books dealing with Italians and Italian Americans and their enormous contributions to America and to civilization. Unfortunately, it wasn't until the end of his career that his studies became recognized.[6]

Finally, Adolfo Caso in "Giovanni Schiavo: Father of Italian-American History" wrote:

> As a historiographer, Giovanni Schiavo is to Italian-American History what Herodotus was to the early Greek world, what Tacitus was to the world of the early Romans, what Villani and Compagni were to the world of the merging Italian republics and city states. Schiavo might be considered the father of Italian-American history, having written the only comprehensive history of a people who have yet to appreciate the rich heritage of the forefathers.[7]

Giovanni Schiavo who died in 1983 was worthy of the above praises. It is unfortunate that such recognition came after his death.

NOTES

1. Originally published in *ComUnico Magazine,* October 2000.
2. Giovanni Schiavo Collection, Research Library of the American–Italian Renaissance Foundation, New Orleans, Louisiana.
3. Sammartino, Peter, *Italian American Digest,* Summer 1983.
4. di Franco, Philip, *The Italian American Experience,* New York, NY: Tom Doherty Associates, 1988.
5. DiNovo, Philip J., "Giovanni Schiavo, Author and Historian," *Il Popolo Italiano,* October 1989.
6. Sorrentino, Anthony, *Organizing the Ethnic Community,* Staten Island, NY: Center for Migration Studies, 1995.

7. Caso, Adolfo, "Giovanni Schiavo: Father of Italian–American History," *Buon Giorno,* August 1998.

CHAPTER 9

SOME IDEAS FOR ITALIAN/AMERICAN RESEARCH IN THE TWENTY-FIRST CENTURY[1]

A large amount of research has been done on Italian Americans throughout the twentieth century. However, continued research, in particular quantitative research, is still needed to better understand the Italian American experience. Such studies can focus on the following topics. It should be stated that some of the following topics can overlap with each other.

1. Italian immigration to the United States after 1965.
Most studies on Italian immigrants in the United States deals with immigrant coming to this country before WWII. How are the Italian immigrants who came after 1965 different from or the same as the Italian immigrants who came before WWII? This research is important for historical documentation.

2. Italian Americans intermarrying with other ethnic groups.
Which groups are the Italian Americans intermarrying with? How are they similar or different from other groups who intermarry in the United States? What cultural traits (if any) are maintained by Italian Americans after marrying outside their ethnic group?

3. Italian American relationship with Jewish Americans, African Americans and Latino/a Americans. A very high percentage of studies involved Italian

American relationship with Irish Americans. The American Italian Historical Association have had conferences dealing with the Italian American relationship with Jewish Americans and African Americans. More research, though, is needed. Many Italian American neighborhoods have been next to Jewish, African and Latino/a American neighborhoods. It is important to study the conflict and cooperation that existed among these groups.

4. Italian/American radicalism.
The John D. Calandra Institute had a conference on Italian American radicalism (just a few years ago). More research, though, is needed on Italian American radicalism in order to give the whole picture on the Italian American political experience. For instance, a special conference could be set up dealing with the life and activities of Antonio Gramsci and Vito Marcantonio.

5. Italian/American female experience.
The majority of studies have been on the Italian American male experience. More studies are needed on the Italian American female experience... For instance, more research is needed on Italian American females working outside the home since a high percentage of Italian American females work outside the home.

6. Occupational and educational achievements of Italian Americans.
Research has been done on the achievements of Italian Americans. However, research on occupational and educational attainments of Italian Americans is continual research. That is, this type of research needs to be to done on a regular basis in order to understand the development of Italian Americans in the United States.

7. The shrinkage and maintenance of Little Italies.
It is important to document the past existence and continued existence of the different Little Italies throughout the United States. It is interesting to examine the reasons for the shrinkage and maintenance of Little Italies. In the Bronx for instance, why are there a noticeable number of Italian American businesses that have existed within the same family for four to five generations?

8. The Italian American suburbs.
A majority of studies deal with Italian Americans in the cities. A very large percentage of Italian Americans live in the suburbs. It is important to examine which cultural traits are maintained by Italian Americans in suburbia and which ones disappear? Which ethnic groups do Italian Americans tend to live with in the suburbs and why?

9. The Italian/American experience in industry, education and the arts.
This research needs to be done on a regular basis in order to a complete understanding of the Italian American experience. False perceptions of Italian Ameri-

cans still persist by the American public (for instance, many Americans view Italian Americans in general as gangsters and/or buffoons). Continued research on the Italian American experience in industry, education and the arts may help dispel such false perceptions.

10. The Italian/American religious experience.
A lot of research has been done on the religious experience of Italian Americans. However, more research is necessary. For instance, it is important to see what religious practices have disappeared among Italian Americans and why? What practices have been maintained? It is also important to examine the religious practices of Italian Americans who are not Catholic?

11. The Italian American middle class.
Most research has been on the Italian American working class. A high percentage of Italian Americans are middle class. It is important to look at which cultural traits have disappeared among middle class Italian Americans and which traits have been maintained by this middle class ethnic group?

12. Prejudice and discrimination toward Italian Americans.
Prejudice and discrimination still exist against Italian Americans. For instance, some studies indicate that many Americans still associate Italian Americans with organized crime (even though, only a fraction of one percent of all Italian Americans are involved in organized crime). More, research is needed to deal with this problem.

It is important that Italian Americans (as well as other ethnic groups) are familiar with their own group's experience and to grasp what is considered productive and practical to shaping their lives. Some of the ideas presented in this chapter may be useful for Italian Americans to become aware of their group's history.

NOTES

1. Originally, unpublished paper presented at "The Italian American Experience in the York City Area Conference," Italian Cultural Center of St. John's University, Jamaica, NY, September 28, 2001.

CHAPTER 10

ITALIAN AMERICAN STUDIES: A GUIDE[1]

"Italian American Studies: A Guide" is a resource for persons interested in studying the Italian American experience. It is broken down into the following sections. Part I lists a number of organizations and journals specializing in Italian American culture. Part II provides a brief description of many leading researchers in the field of Italian American studies.

Part I
Organizations and Journals Specializing in Italian American Studies
This section lists a number of organizations and journals that publish and/or provide awards for works specializing in Italian American research. It also lists organizations that sponsor lecture series in Italian American studies.

American Italian Historical Association
209 Flagg Place
Staten Island, NY 10304
An interdisciplinary organization dedicated to Italian American studies. Sponsors annual conferences to present scholarly papers. Publishes proceeding form conferences. Offers a scholarships of $500.00 to a graduate student, in any discipline, whose work focuses on the Italian American experience.

Arba Sicula
Modern Foreign languages
St. John's University,
Jamaica, NY 11439.
Contact: Prof. Gaetano Cipolla

A non-profit international cultural organization. Promotes Sicilian culture. Publishes *Arba Sicula*, a bilingual (Sicilian-English) journal that focuses on the folklore and the literature of Sicily and her people all over the world.

John D. Calandra Italian American Institute
25 West 43rd Street, Suite 1000
New York, NY 10036
Contact: Dr. Vincenzo Milione
(212) 642-2095
Sponsors conferences on local, national and international levels for both academic and public audiences. Collects data on Italian American educational and occupational attainment. Serves as a research depository of information and support. Provides research opportunities for national and international faculty and students. Develops grants for research funding. Publishes reports and monographs on Italian American studies, and *The Italian American Review, A Social Science Journal of the Italian American Experience. The Italian American Review* also awards The Massaro Prize of $500.00 for the best article appearing in the journal that responds to an historical, social or political theme.

Center for Italian Studies
State University of New York
Stony Brook, New York, 11794-3358
Contact: Dr. Fred Gardaphe, Director of the Center for Italian Studies.

Center for Migration Studies
209 Flagg Place
Staten Island, NY 10304-1199
Tel. (718) 351-8800
Publishes monographs and books on Italian American culture, sociology and the arts, critical and creative. Submit Manuscripts to: Lydio F. Tomasi, Executive Director of the Center.

Com. It. Es (Committee of Italians Abroad)
22 East 38th Street, Suite 300
New York, NY 10016
Tel: (212) 532-8311
Contact: Dr. Silvana Mangione
Sponsors: Lecture Series.

Enrico Fermi Cultural Center
610 East 187th St.
Bronx, NY 10458
(718) 933-6410
Sponsors lecture series and contains data on files for research on the Italian American experience.

Italian Americana
A semi-annual historical and cultural journal devoted to the Italian experience in America. Submit papers (20 double-spaced pages maximum) to:
Carol Bonomo Albright, Editor
Italian Americana
URI/CCE
80 Washington St.
Providence, RI 02903
Italian Americana also awards the following annual prizes for the best poetry and article appearing in the journal: $1,000 John Ciardi Poetry Prize (Sponsor: National Italian American Foundation), $250 Bruno Acrudi Short Fiction Awards and $250 A. William Salamone History Award.

The Italian American Review
A Social Science Journal of the Italian American Experience. Submit manuscripts (25 double-spaced pages maximum) to:
Philip V. Cannistraro, Editor, IAR
The John D. Calandra Italian American Institute
Queens College/CUNY
25 West 43rd Street, Suite 1000
New York, NY 10036
The Italian American Review awards The Massaro Prize ($500) for the best article appearing in the journal.

Italian/American Studies
Fred Gardaphe, Editor
Write to SUNY Press
State University Plaza
Albany, NY 12246
Publishes books on Italian American culture.

Italian Cultural Center
The Institute for Italian Heritage and Culture of St. John's University. The Center plans to set up a lecture series, a millennium series and a scholarship program.

National Italian American Foundation
NIAF Education Director
666 11th St.
N.W., Washington, DC, 20001
Tel. (202) 638-0220
The National Italian American Foundation provides scholarships, grants and fellowships.

UNICO Foundation
72 Burroughs Place
Bloomfield, NJ, 07003-3496
The UNICO Foundation provides national scholarship awards and the National
Ella T. Grasso Literary Awards. UNICO is the largest Italian American service
organizations in the United States. *ComUnico Magazine* is the official publica-
tion of the UNICO Foundation.
Tel (973) 748-7202

VIA
Voices in Italian Americana. A literary and cultural review essays, fiction and
non-fiction should not exceed twenty pages, poetry five pages. Typewritten and
double spaced. Submit to:
Fred Gardaphe
Center for Italian Studies
State University of New York
Stony Brook, NY 11793-3358
Voices in Italian Americana is a semiannual literary and cultural review devoted
to the dissemination of information concerning the contributions of and about
Italian Americans of North America. *Voices in Italian Americana* awards the
Aniello Lauri Award ($150) for the best creative work appearing in VIA and the
Massaro Award ($500) for the best critical essay appearing in VIA on a histori-
cal theme.

VIA Folios
Bordighera Incorporated
PO Box 1374
Lafayette, IN 47902-1374
VIA Folios is a refereed "small-book" series published by Bordighera, Inc. dedi-
cated to critical studies on Italian and Italian/American culture. VIA Folios also
publishes works of poetry, fiction, theater and translations from Italian. Inter-
ested authors should write to the editors before submitting an entire manuscript.

Editors
Fred L. Gardaphe
Center for Italian Studies
State University of New York
Stony Brook, NY 11794-3358
E-mail: fgar@aol.com

Paolo A. Giordano
Modern Languages & Literature
Loyola University
Chicago, IL 60625
E-mail: pgiora@orion.it.luc.edu

Anthony Julian Tamburri
Foreign Languages & Literature
Purdue University
West Lafayette, IN 47906-1359
E-mail: tamburri@purdue.edu

Part II

Scholars in the Field of Italian American Studies

This section provides a list of many leading scholars in the field of Italian American studies, their affiliation and a brief biography.

Richard Alba

State University of New York at Albany
Author of *Italian Americans into the Twilight of Ethnicity* (Prentice Hall, 1985). Studies focus on ethnicity in the United States.

Carol Bonomo Albright

University of Rhode Island-Providence
Editor of *Italian Americana.* Research deals with the Italian American experience.

Helen Barolini

American Italian Historical Association
Author of *Chiaroscuro: Essays of Identity* (Bordighera, 1997). Publications deal with Italian American women.

Lucia Chiavola Birnbaum

Stanford University
Author of *Liberazone della Donna: Feminism in Italy* (Wesleyan University Press, 1986). Has published on the Sicilian and Sicilian American female experience.

Mary Jo Bona

Gonzaga University
Co-edited Through the Looking Glass (American Italian Historical Association, 1996). Works focus on the Italian American female experience.

Dominic Candeloro

American Italian Historical Association
President of the American Italian Historical Association, 1985 to 1988. Co-edited *Italian Ethnics: Their Language, Literature and Life,* American Italian Historical Association, 1990. Research deals with Italian American culture.

Philip V. Cannistraro
Queens College/CUNY
Editor of the *Italian American Review (IAR): A Social Science Journal of the Italian American Experience.* Co-edited *Italian Americans: The Search for a Usable Past* (American Italian Historical Association, 1989). Has done research on the Italian American experience.

Rocco Caporale
St. John's University
Editor of *The Italian Americans through the Generations* (American Italian Historical Association, 1977). Studies focus on Italian Americans.

Betty Boyd Caroli
Kingsborough Community College, CUNY
Co-edited *The Italian Immigrant Woman in North America* (American Italian Historical Association, 1977). Studies focus on Italian Americans.

Frank Cavaioli
State University College at Farmingdale, New York
President of the American Italian Historical Association 1983-1984. Co-edited *Italian Americans and their Public and Private Life* (American Italian Historical Association, 1993). Publications focus on many aspects of the Italian American Experience.

Gaetano Cipolla
St. John's University
Editor of *Arba Sicula.* Has done research on Sicily and Sicilians in America.

Vaneeta-marie D'Andrea
University of Connecticut
Publications deal with the Italian American female experience.

William V. D'Antonio
Catholic University of America
Has published and lectured on Italian Americans.

Angela Danzi
SUNY Farmingdale
Co-edited *Italian Americans and their Public and Private Life* (American Italian Historical Association, 1993). Research deals with the Italian American experience.

Judith DeSena
St. John's University

Co-edited *Italian Americans in a Multicultural Society* (American Italian Historical Association, 1994). Interest is in the activities of working class women in ethnic neighborhoods, particularly in Italian American neighborhoods.

William Egelman
Iona College
Co-edited *The Melting Pot and Beyond: Italian Americans in the Year 2000* (American Italian Historical Association, 1987). Research deals with the occupational and educational attainments of Italian Americans.

Francis X. Femminella
State University of New York at Albany
President of the American Italian Historical Association, 1981-1982. Edited *Power and Class: The Italian American Experience Today* (American Italian Historical Association, 1971) and edited *The Interaction of Italians and Irish in the United States* (American Italian Historical Association, 1985). Has published in the field of Italian American studies.

Richard Gambino
Queens College, City University of New York
Author of *Blood of My Blood: The Dilemma of the Italian-American* (Doubleday, 1974) and *Vendetta: The Story of the Largest Lynching in American History* (Doubleday, 1977). Research deals with Italian American society.

Fred Gardaphe
State University of New York –Stony Brook
Current president of the American Italian Hisotrical Association. Cofounder and review editor of *Voices in Italian Americana (VIA)*. Director of the Center for Italian Studies, SUNY, Stony Brook. Publications focus on Italian American literature.

Louis Gesualdi
St, John's University
Author of *The Italian Immigrants of Connecticut, 1880-1940* (Connecticut Academy of Arts and Sciences, 1997) and *The Religious Acculturation of the Italian American Catholics: Cultural and Socioeconomic Factors* (Calandra Institute, CUNY, 1997). Has published on the Italian American experience.

Luciano J. Iorrizzo
State University of New York- Oswego
President of the American Italian Historical Association, 1975-1978. Edited *An Inquiry into Organized Crime* (American Italian Historical Association, 1970). Has published on Italian Americans.

Paola A. Sensi Isolani
Saint Mary's College of California
Co-edited *Italian American Celebrate Life: The Arts and Popular Culture* (American Italian Historical Association, 1990). Has done research in Southern Italy and among Italian Americans in the United States.

Richard Juliani
Villanova University
President of the American Italian Historical Association, 1989-1992. Author Of *Building Little Italy* (Penn State University, 1998). Has edited books for the American Italian Historical Association and published articles on Italian Americans.

Jerome Krase
Brooklyn College of the City University of New York
President of the American Italian Historical Association, 1993-1994. Co-edited *The Melting Pot and Beyond: Italian Americans in the Year 2000* (American Italian Historical Association, 1989) and *Italian Americans in Multicultural Society* (American Italian Historical Association, 1994). Has written and lectured on Italian American affairs.

Salvatore LaGumina
Nassau County Community College
President of the American Italian Historical Association, 1971-74. Co-edited *Italian Americans and their Public and Private Life* (American Italian Historical Association, 1973). Has authored books and articles dealing with Italian Americans.

Anthony L. LaRuffa
Lehman College
Director of Italian American Studies at Lehman College. Author of *Monte Carmelo: An Italian Community in the Bronx* (Gordon and Breach Science Publishers, 1988).

Joseph Lopreato
University of Texas, Austin
Author of *Peasants No More* (Chandler Publishing Co., 1967) and *Italian Americans* (Random House, 1970). Has done research on Italians and Italian Americans.

Margherita Marchione
Farleigh Dickinson University
Director of the Salvatore Center for Mazzei Studies. Author of *Philip Mazzei: Jefferson's "Zealous Whig"* (American Institue of Italian Studies, 1975). Studies deal with the Italian American experience.

Elizabeth Mathias
St. John's University
Co-authored *Italian Folktales in America: The Verbal Art of an Immigrant Woman* (Wayne State University, 1985). Research deals with Italians in Southern Italy and Italian immigrants in the United States.

Vincenzo Milione
Calandfra Italian American Institute—CUNY
Director for Rearch and Education, Calandra Institute, CUNY. Has published reports and articles on the educational and occupational attainments of Italian Americans.

Humbert S. Nelli
University of Kentucky
Authored *The Italians in Chicago, 1880-1930* (Oxford University Press, 1970) and edited *The United States and Italy: The First Two Hundred Years* (American Italian Historical Association, 1977). Has written on Italian American society.

Emiliana Noether
University of Connecticut
Has held and attained several fellowships and grants. Research is on the Italian American experience.

George E. Pozzetta
University of Florida
President of the American Italian Historical Association, 1979-1980. Edited *Pane E Lavoro: The Italian American Working Class* (American Italian Historical Association, 1978. Has authored works on Italian immigration.

Joseph Scelsa
Calandra Italian American Institute, CUNY
Executive Director of the Calandra Institute, CUNY. Co-edited *Italian Americans in Transition* (American Italian Historical Association, 1990). Has published reports and articles on Italian Americans.

Anthony Tamburri
Purdue University
Cofounder – Editor of *Voices in Italian Americana (VIA)*. Co-edited *Italian Americans Celebrate Life: The Arts and Popular Culture* (American Italian Historical Association, 1990).

Lydio Tomasi
Director of the Center for Migration Studies – Staten Island

Author of *The Italian American Family* (Center for Migration Studies, Staten Island, 1972). Publications focus on Italian American studies.

Sylvano Tomasi
Center for Migration Studies- Staten Island
Edited *The Religious Experience of Italian Americans* (American Italian Historical Association, 1973). Author of *Piety and Power* (Center for Migration Studies-Staten Island, 1972).

Donald Tricarico
Queensborough Community College
Author of *The Italians of Greenwich Village: The Social Structure and Transformation of an Ethnic Community* (Center for Migration Studies-Staten Island, 1984). Research deals with Italian Americans in New York City.

Joseph Varacalli
Nassau Community College
Has written in the area of Italian American and American Catholic studies.

Rudolph Vecoli
University of Minnesota
President of the American Italian Historical Association. Director of the Immigration History Research Center at the University of Minnesota. Edited *Italian American Radicalism: Old World Origins and New World Developments* (American Italian Historical Association, 1987). Has done research on Italian immigrants in America.

Patricia Snyder Weibust
University of Connecticut
Co-Director of the Isaac N. Thut World Education Center at the University of Connecticut. Prepared with two co-authors, *The Italians, In their Homeland, In America, In Connecticut* (University of Connecticut, 1976).

NOTES

1. Originally published by the Center for Global Education, St. John's University, Jamaica, NY, 1999.

CHAPTER 11

THE ITALIAN/AMERICAN EXPERIENCE: AN ANNOTATED BIBLIOGRAPHY[1]

There exist many books about the Italian and the Italian American experience of the twentieth century. However, as we begin the twenty–first century, continued research is still necessary in order to understand the lives of Italian Americans. Future studies need to deal with the following: 1) Quantitative research on the lives of Italians and Italian Americans, in general; 2) Italian American organizations, past and present; 3) New forms of Italian American communities in the cities and suburbs; 4) Italian immigration to the United States after 1965; 5) The religious life of Italians and Italian Americans; 6) The experiences of Italian and Italian American women; 7) Changes in the lives of Italians in Southern Italy and Italian Americans in the United States during the last one hundred fifty years; 8) Italian American professionals; 9) The experiences of the third, fourth and fifth generation Italian Americans; 10) Italian Americans intermarrying with other groups; 11) Italian Americans in industry, work, politics, education and the arts; 12) The Italian American poor, working class, middle class, upper middle class and elite class; 13) The continued prejudice and discrimination experienced by Italian Americans; 14) Historical, sociological and/or psychological accounts of Italian Americans of the seventeenth, eighteenth, nineteenth and twenty centuries; and 15) Expectations and predictions for Italian Americans in the Twenty–first century.

This work is an annotated bibliography of some key books dealing with the lives of Italians and Italian Americans. It is a resource for persons interested in studying the Italian/American experience.

Annotated Bibliography

Abramson, Harold, J. *Ethnic Diversity in Catholic America.* New York, NY: John Wiley and Sons, 1973.

Abramson's study describes the ethnic diversity in religious behavior that exists among the Catholic Americans (this includes Italian–American Catholics). This book argues that the different Catholic ethnic groups maintain cultural traits that were developed in their respective countries of origin. It states that the differences in religious behavior among the different Catholic ethnic groups are an outcome of the maintenance of cultural traits.

Alba, Richard. *Italian–Americans into the Twilight of Ethnicity.* Englewood Cliffs, NJ: Prentice–Hall, Inc., 1985.

Richard Alba indicates the profound changes which occurred among Italian–Americans during the twentieth century. These changes include the loss of the Italian language by the third generation; the dispersion of Italian immigrant communities; a considerable economic and occupational mobility of this group over the past decades; the erosion of past cultural values; and the Italian–Americans' accelerating rates of intermarriage with other ethnic and religious groups. The author demonstrates that ethnic traits associated with Italian–Americans are disappearing and that this disappearance is an outcome of socio-economic conditions existing in the United States.

American Italian Historical Association Publications of Proceedings. Staten Island, NY: American Italian Historical Association, Volumes 1 to 30 from 1968 to 1999.

The American Italian Historical Association is an interdisciplinary organization dedicated to Italian American studies. It sponsors annual conferences to present scholarly papers on the Italian American experience and publishes the proceedings from the conferences.

Volume 1   *Ethnicity in American Political Life: The Italian American Case.* Edited by Salvatore J. LaGumina (1968).

Volume 2   *The Italian American Novel.* Edited by John M. Cammett (1969).

Volume 3   *An Inquiry into Organized Crime.* Edited by Luciano J. Iorizzo (1970).

Volume 4   *Power and Class: The Italian American Experience Today.* Edited By Frances X. Femminella (1971).

Volume 5   *Italian American Radicalism: Old World Origins and New World Developments.* Edited by Rudolph J. Vecoli (1972).

Volume 6   *The Religious Experience of Italian Americans.* Edited by Silvano Tomasi (1973).

Volume 7   *The Interaction of Italians and Jews in America.* Edited by Jean Scarpaci (1974).

Volume 8   *The Urban Experience of Italian Americans.* Edited by Pat Gallo (1975).

Volume 9   *The United States and Italy: The First Two Hundred Years.* Edited by Humbert Nelli (1976).

Volume 10   *The Italian Immigrant Woman in North America.* Edited by Betty Boyd Caroli, Robert Harney, and Lydio F. Tomasi (1977).

Volume 11   *Pane e Lavoro: The Italian American Working Class.* Edited by George E. Pozzetta (1978).

Volume 12   *Italian Americans in the Professions.* Edited by Remegio U. Pane (1983).

Volume 13   *The Family and Community Life of Italian Americans.* Edited by Richard N. Juliani (1983).

Volume 14   *Italian Immigrants in Rural and Small Town America.* Edited by Rudolph J. Vecoli (1987).

Volume 15   *The Italian Americans Through the Generations: The First One Hundred Years.* Edited by Rocco Caporale (1986).

Volume 16   *The Interaction of Italians and Irish in the United States.* Edited by Francis X. Femminella (1985).

Volume 17   *Italian Americans: Struggle and Support.* Edited by Joseph L. Tropea, James E. Miller, and Cheryl Beattie Repetti (1986).

Volume 18   *The Melting Pot and Beyond: Italian Americans in the Year 2000.* Edited by Jerome Krase and William Egelman (1987).

Volume 19   *Italian Americans: The Search for a Usable Past.* Edited by Richard N. Juliani and Philip V. Cannistraro (1989).

Volume 20   *Italian Ethnics: Their Languages, Literature and Life.* Edited by Dominic Candeloro, Fred Gardaphe, and Paolo Giordano (1990).

Volume 21   *Italian Americans in Transition.* Edited by Joseph Scelsa, Salvatore J. LaGumina and Lydio F. Tomasi (1990).

Volume 22   *Italian Americans Celebrate Life.* Edited by Paola A. Sensi Isolani and Anthony Julian Tamburri (1990).

Volume 23   *A Century of Italian Immigration, 1890–1990.* Edited by Harral Landry (1994).

Volume 24   *Italian Americans and Their Public and Private Life.* Edited by Frank J.Cavaioli, Angela Danzi, and Salvatore J. LaGumina (1993).

Volume 25   *New Explorations in Italian American Studies.* Edited by Richard N. Juliani and Sandra P. Juliani (1994).

Volume 26   *Italian Americans in a Multicultural Society.* Edited by Jerome Krase and Judith N. DeSena (1994).

Volume 27   *Through the Looking Glass: Italian and Italian/American Images in the Media.* Edited by Mary Jo Bona and Anthony Julian Tamburri (1996).

Volume 28   *Industry, Technology, Labor and the Italian American Communities.* Edited by Mario Aste, Jerome Krase, Louise Napolitano–Carman and Janet E. Worrall (1997).

Volume 29   *A Tavola: Food, Tradition and Community Among Italian Americans.* Edited by Edvige Giunta and Sam Patti (1998).

Volume 30   *Shades of Black and White Conflict and Collaboration Between Two Communities.* Edited by Dan Ashyk, Fred L. Gardaphe and Anthony Julian Tamburri (1999).

Amfitheatrof, Erik. *The Children of Columbus: An Informal History of the Italians in the New World.* Boston, MA: Little, Brown and Company, 1973.

Amfitheatrof's book describes the first Italian explorers who came to the Americas and it presents a historical account of rural Italy. His book is also about Italian–Americans both unassuming and distinguished, whose experience is key in the development of the United States. This work dispels the many Italian–American stereotypes that exist in our nation.

Balboni, Alan Richard. *Beyond the Mafia: Italian Americans and the Development of Las Vegas.* Reno, NV: University of Nevada Press, 1996.

Balboni's work describes how Italian–Americans who were not involved in illegal operations contributed to the development of Las Vegas from a desert town into a well–known resort city. This book provides a detailed explanation of the Italian–American experience in a wide range of civic, professional and business activities.

Banfield, Edward, C. *The Moral Basis of a Backward Society.* New York, NY: The Free Press, 1958.

Banfield's book *The Moral Basis of a Backward Society* describes a Southern Italian town in Southern Italy with emphasis on its political behavior. It depicts the social life of this town lacking in moral sanctions outside those of the immediate family. The Southern Italians were shown to be reluctant to cooperation and to any kind of continuing relationship beyond the nuclear family. To explain this behavior, Banfield argues that the people from Southern Italy behave at all times as if they were following a rule that he called amoral familism: "Maximize the material, short–run advantage of the nuclear family, assume that all others will do likewise."

Barzini, Luigi. *The Italian.* New York, NY: Atheneum Publishers, 1964.

Barzini's book describes the manners, morals and behavior of the Italian people. In particular, the work examines the power of the Italian family. It points out the importance to protect, improve, honor and fear the family by the employment of whatever necessary methods.

Battistella, Graziano (editor). *Italian Americans in the 80s: A Sociodemographic Profile.* Staten Island, NY: Center for Migration Studies, 1989.

Battistella's volume presents a set of unpublished data on Italian Americans that was prepared by the United States Bureau of the Census. This book contains works dealing with the Italian immigrants to the United States in the 1970s and 80s, demographic and cultural aspects of Italian–Americans, education, family life and economic characteristics of Italian–Americans in the 1980s.

Bell, Rudolph B. *Fate and Honor, Family and Village: Demographic and Cultural Change in Rural Italy Since 1800.* Chicago, IL: University of Chicago Press, 1979.

Bell analyzes the extreme poverty and deprivation that exist in Calabria, Italy. He describes the unhappy physical and moral state known as *la miseria* (the misery) of the peasants in Southern Italy.

Belliotti, Raymond A. *Seeking Identity: Individualism versus Community in an Ethnic Context.* Lawrence, KS: University Press of Kansas, 1995.

Belliotti's volume argues that the Italian–Americans of the 1990s have continued to view themselves as a particular ethnic group, still separate to some degree from mainstream American culture. The book maintains that anti–Italian bias and stereotypes still prevent today's Italian–Americans from being fully assimilated to American culture.

Biagiotti, Aldo P. *Impact: The Historical Account of the Italian Immigrants of Ridgefield, Connecticut.* Ridgefield, CT: Romald Press, 1990.

Biagiotti's book explains the lives of Italian immigrants in Ridgefield, Connecticut from the early 1900s to the 1940s. This work describes these immigrants' experiences during the prohibition era, the Great Depression and World War II. It also examines the discrimination against the Italian immigrants of Ridgefield and the mutual aid society, nicknames and sayings of this group.

Bianco, Carla. *The Two Rosetos.* Bloomington, IN: Indiana University Press, 1974.

Bianco's book describes the trials and tribulations of Italian immigrants from Roseto Valfortore (a village in Foggia, Apulia) in Roseto, Pennsylvania. This work examines the manner in which the traditional life firmly established in Italy was triumphantly transferred and continued in the United States. Traditional attitudes toward the family, government and religion were maintained and grew in Pennsylvania.

Block, Anton. *The Mafia of a Sicilian Village, 1860–1960.* Prospect Heights, IL: Waveland Press, 1971.

Block's study on the Mafia in Sicily indicates that it was never a highly structured criminal conspiracy. This work shows that the Mafia in Sicily was a mediator and fractional operation of mercenaries arranging local subjugation of the peasantry for absentee landlords.

Bohme, Frederick G. *A History of the Italians in New Mexico.* New York, NY: Arno Press, 1975.

Bohme's work provides a description of the Italian American experience in New Mexico from 1850 to 1950. The book discusses the importance of the Italian settlers as mediators between the Anglo–Saxon and Hispanic culture in New Mexico.

Briggs, John Walker. *An Italian Passage: Immigrants to Three American Cities, 1870– 1930.* New Haven, CT: Yale University, 1978.

Briggs' book examines the Italian communities in Utica and Rochester, New York and in Kansas City, Missouri during the migration period of 1880 to 1920 to America. It indicates that the Italian immigrants' ideas concerning self–help, group organization, social mobility, and the economic value of education which was developed in Southern Italy had become very useful to them in America. This work points out that once the Italians had decided to stay in America and not return to Italy after having accumulated some money, they began achieving social and economic success in the United States while maintaining their cultural traditions.

Bruhn, John, G. and Wolf, Stewart. *The Roseto Story: An Anatomy of Health.* Norman, OK: University of Oklahoma Press, 1979.

Bruhn and Wolf's study investigates the Italian community of Roseto, Pennsylvania. The book's findings indicate that a close connection to an Italian–American ethnic way of life has been of great benefit to the physical and mental health of the people of Roseto.

Buhle, Paul and Georgakas, Dan. (editors). *The Immigrant Left in the United States.* Albany, NY: State University Press, 1997.

Buhle and Georgakas' work includes essays on Mexican–, German–, Jewish–, Italian–, Polish–, Ukrainian–, Greek–, Haitian–, Arab– and Asian–Americans. These essays provide information on the roles the Left (that is, radical politics) has played among these ethnic groups.

Child, Irvin, *Italian or American? The Second Generation in Conflict.* New Haven, CT: Yale University Press, 1943.

Irvin Child, who studied the second generation of Italian–Americans in the 1940s, found three different reactions of this group in their adjustment to American culture: the rebel reaction (the person wants to become fully American and rejects fully his/her Italian identification), the in–group reaction (the person strives to strengthen his/her identity as an Italian) and the apathetic reaction (the person compromises the American way of life with the Italian way). The last person here is in a sense apathetic in that he/she is unwilling to be a fully committed American nor a fully committed Italian.

Churchill, Charles Wesley. *The Italians of Newark: A Community Study.* New York, NY: Arno Press, 1975.

Churchill's work on the Italian community in Newark was based on interviews of 700 Italian Americans during the late 1930s. The book discusses the

Italian Americans' work, family life, religion and the Church, political life, organizations, education and opinions.

Cinel, Dino. *From Italy to San Francisco: The Immigrant Experience.* Palo Alto, CA: Stanford University Press, 1982.

Cinel's book is a study of a 2000 family sample of Italians who migrated to San Francisco from the 1850s to the 1930s. The work describes the ambivalence, perplexity and conflict of the Italian immigrants in San Francisco.

Colletta, John Philip. *Finding Italian Roots.* Baltimore, MD: Genealogical Publishing Co., Inc., 1993.

Colletta's book is a guide to Italian genealogy for Americans. It provides a detailed description of records of genealogical value in Italy. This guide also contains a glossary of key Italian words and an extensive annotated bibliography.

Cordasco, Francesco. *Italian Americans: A Guide to Information Sources.* Detroit, MI: Gale Research Co., 1978.

Cordasco provides an extensive bibliography of works available on all aspects of the Italian experience in the United States. This work includes materials covering history, social science, literature, and health of the Italian–Americans.

Cordasco, Francesco (editor). *Studies in Italian American Social History: Essays in Honor of Leonard Covello.* Totowa, NJ: Rowman and Littlefield, 1975.

Cordasco's book is a collection of original essays on the Italian experience in the United States. This volume contains essays that deal with such topics as conflict, acculturation, assimilation, anti Fascist reactions in the United States, the Italian language press, the Italian immigrant woman, early Italian political refugees, and the patterns of Italian emigration.

Cordasco, Francesco and Bucchioni, Eugene (editors). *The Italians: Social Backgroundsof an American Group.* Clifton, NJ: Augustus M. Kelley, Publishers, 1974.

Cordasco and Bucchioni's sourcebook is a collection of materials on the Italian–American experience from 1890 to 1940. This text examines this group's emigration, communities in America, responses to American life, employment, health, social needs and education.

Covello, Leonard. *The Sociological Background of the Italo American School Child.* Leiden, Netherlands: E. J. Brill, 1967.

Leonard Covello stated that education to the Italian parent (that is, Southern Italian peasant) was the teaching of society's cultural, social and moral values to the child by the parents. The Italian peasant, according to Covello, in order to maintain the Southern Italian way of life opposed education from outside the family. He indicated that the Italian's mistrust of school was developed in Southern Italy and was maintained in America.

Crispino, James. *The Assimilation of Ethnic Groups: The Italian Case.* Staten Island, NY: Center for Migration Studies, 1980.

Crispino's study documents the assimilation process as it applies to Italian–Americans. This book examines the roles of friendship, marriage partner selection and religion in the Italian community of Bridgeport, Connecticut. It describes the extent to which the Italian–Americans of this city have acculturated to the larger American society's culture and value system.

Cronin, Constance. *The Sting of Change: Sicilians in Sicily and Australia.* Chicago, IL: University of Chicago Press, 1970.

Cronin's work examines the Sicilian family in Sicily and in Australia. The book discusses the unity of the Sicilian nuclear family. It points out that when disagreements occur with outsiders, the nuclear family acts as sole unit safekeeping and strengthening its own against the others.

Del Giudice, Luisa (editor). *Studies in Italian American Folklore.* Logan, UT: Utah State Press, 1993.

Del Giudice's book is a collection of essays by different authors on Italian American folklife. These essays focus on both new and old immigrants from the largely post–World War II community in Toronto, Canada to the more established Italian Americans of New York and Philadelphia.

DeMarco, William M. *Ethnics and Enclaves: Boston's Italian North End.* Ann Arbor, MI: UMI Research Press, 1981.

DeMarco's work examines the housing, marriage, religious and employment patterns of the Italian Americans from the North End community in Boston from the 1870s to 1930. The study provides an explanation for the values of the Italian Americans of this community.

Diggins, John P. *Mussolini and Fascism: The View from America.* Princeton, NJ: Princeton University Press, 1972.

Diggins' book demonstrates that during the 1920s and 1930s most Americans were captivated by Mussolini and approved of Fascism. This work indicates that the American press at that time period presented Mussolini in a positive light, and being pro–Mussolini was very mainstream.

Dolci, Danilo. *Sicilian Lives.* New York, NY: Pantheon Books, 1981.

Dolci's work examines the economics, politics and social lives of the people from Sicily. The book reveals confidential experiences and insights of a large range of Sicilians, rural and urban.

Fucilla, Joseph G. *Our Italian Surnames.* Baltimore, MD: Genealogical Publishing Co., Inc.,1987.

Fucilla's book deals with the origins and history of Italian surnames. It attempts to classify and derive Italian surnames on the basis of all the available evidence.

Gallo, Patrick J., *Ethnic Alienation: The Italian–Americans.* Rutherford, NJ: Farleigh Dickinson University Press, 1974.

Gallo's study examines the political behavior of three generations of Italian–Americans. This book attempts to make clear the prominence of ethnicity in the political viewpoints of Italian–Americans, and the politically pertinent decisions they make.

Gallo, Patrick J. *Old Bread, New Wine: A Portrait of the Italian–Americans.* Chicago, IL: Nelson–Hall, 1981.

Gallo's book is an interdisciplinary study of Italian–Americans. This work examines life in Italy, the Italian family, and the religious experience of Italians and Italian–Americans. It also investigates the problems experienced by Italian–Americans as a result of living in urban America.

Gambino, Richard. *Blood of My Blood: The Dilemma of the Italian–Americans.* Garden City, NY: Anchor Press/Doubleday, 1974.

Gambino argues that the Italian–Americans' lack of participation in organizations is an outcome of their family attitudes (that is, a mistrust of organizations outside the family, including educational organizations and the Catholic Church). The author states that because of their negative attitude toward schooling and their desire to remain close to the family, Italian–Americans have gone into blue–collar rather than white–collar work.

Gambino, Richard. *Vendetta: The Story of the Largest Lynching in American History.* Garden City, NY: Doubleday, 1977.

Gambino describes the largest lynching in American history that took place in New Orleans on March 14, 1891. The victims, who were eleven Italian Americans, were pulled out of prison and executed by a lynch mob of approximately 20,000 people. No one was brought to justice in any way for the mob brutality.

Gans, Herbert. *The Urban Villagers: Group and Class in the Life of Italian–Americans.* New York, NY: The Free Press, 1962.

Gans' work is a participant–observation study of the West End section of Boston, and in particular, of the second generation Italian–Americans who lived there. The book demonstrates that the Italian–Americans' way of life in the West End was made up of a particular and independent working–class sub–culture. It indicates that ethnicity was of lower significance in explaining Italian–American behavior than class.

Gelorimino, A. Gerald and Gotti, Margaret R. *The Italian Heritage in Yonkers.* Yonkers, NY: Gazette Press, Inc. Publishers, 1986.

Gelorimino and Gottis's book describes the contribution that Italian Americans have made to the social, political, cultural and economic life of Yonkers, NY. This work is a representation of the diversity, life and significant presence of Italian Americans in the city of Yonkers. The text looks at the disadvantages and prejudices experienced by these Italian Americans. It also examines this ethnic group's family influences, religion, organizations and education in Yonkers.

Gesualdi, Louis. *The Italian Immigrants of Connecticut, 1880 to 1940.* New Haven, CT: The Connecticut Academy of Arts and Sciences, 1997.

Gesualdi's study indicates that many Italian immigrants who lived in the cities of Connecticut from 1880 to 1940 had a mistrust of outsiders' attitude at least to some degree. These Italian immigrants had experienced harsh socioeconomic conditions in Southern Italy and in Connecticut. These socioeconomic conditions influenced the development of a mistrust of outsiders' attitude among these Italians and this group's failure to participate in various organizations and institutions.

Giordano, Joseph (editor). *The Italian–American Catalog: A Lavish and Loving Celebration of and Guide to Our Culture, History, Neighborhoods, Family, Food and Drink.* New York, NY: Doubleday and Company, Inc., 1986.

Giordano's book offers an informative look at the lives of Italian–Americans. This work contains essays written by different people that describe the family, neighborhood, food and drink, culture and history of Italian–Americans.

Glazer, Nathan. *Ethnic Dilemmas. 1964–1982.* Cambridge, MA: Harvard University, 1983.

Glazer's book examines ethnic self–consciousness and affirmative action policies. This work discusses the reoccurring rise and fall of ethnicity as an issue in American politics and culture. It describes the differences between blacks and white ethnic groups (including Italian–Americans).

Glazer Nathan and Moynihan Daniel P. *Beyond the Melting Pot: The Negroes, Puerto Ricans, Jews, Italians and Irish of New York City.* Cambridge, MA: M. I. T. Press, 1963.

Glazer and Moynihan's study describes the experiences of the African Americans, Puerto Rican Americans, Jewish Americans, Italian Americans and Irish Americans in New York City. This work argues that ethnicity in New York is important and that it would continue to be an important part of politics and culture.

Greeley, Andrew M. *The American Catholic: A Social Portrait.* New York, NY: Basic Books, Inc., Publishers, 1977.

Greeley's study deals with the latter stages of the acculturation of the Catholic ethnic immigrant groups (including Italian–American Catholics) into American society. It examines the educational attainment, family patterns, income achievement, moral values, occupational prestige and political behavior of the American Catholic groups.

Greeley, Andrew M. *Ethnicity in the United States.* New York, NY: Wiley, 1974.

Greeley's work tested people from Irish, Italian and British backgrounds with respect to these groups' differences in attitudes. It argues that cultural differences exist among these ethnic groups.

Greeley, Andrew M. *Why Can't They Be Like Us?: America's White Ethnic Groups.* New York, NY: Dutton, 1971.

Greeley's study claims that there exist differences in behavior by the different white ethnic groups (including Italian–Americans) in the United States. It maintains that the knowledge of a group's heritage is necessary to comprehend their behavior.

Grossman Ronald P. *The Italians in America.* Minneapolis, MN: Lerner Publications, 1975.

Grossman's work provides an outlook of the history of Italians in the United States. This book cites a selection of famous Italian Americans.

Gumina, Deanna Paoli. *The Italians of San Francisco (1850–1930).* Staten Island, NY: Center for Migration Studies, 1977.

Gumina's book describes the Italian American experience from the point of view of the Italian immigrants who migrated to California. It examines the economic and social aspects of the Italian migratory experience and settlement in San Francisco from 1850 to 1930.

Harney, Robert F. and Scarpaci, J. Vincenza (editors). *Little Italies in North America.* Toronto, ON: The Multicultural History Society of Ontario, 1981.

Harney and Scarpaci's volume consists of essays that examine the Little Italies in Chicago, New York, Philadelphia, Baltimore, Oswego, Tampa, New Orleans, St. Louis, Toronto and Montreal. These essays provide an explanation for the development and location of the Italian communities in Canada and the United States. This work investigates the culture and society of these Little Italies.

Ianni, Francis A. J. *A Family Business.* New York, NY: Mentor, 1972.

Ianni indicates that Prohibition became the source for power and profit that allowed an American Mafia to form. Prior to prohibition, Black Hand activities were focused on robbery, extortion, and other traditional, low–profit crimes within the Italian community.

Immerso, Michael. *Newark's Little Italy: The Vanished First Ward.* New Brunswick, NJ: Rutgers University Press, 1997.

Immerso's work describes a period of over 70 years, from the settlement of the first Southern Italian immigrants in Newark's Little Italy in the 1880s to the arrival of the bulldozers that tore down this neighborhood. This community was cleared for a massive urban renewal project of hi rise public housing buildings. Newark's Little Italy was completely gone by the 1970s. The book is a description of the families, St. Lucy's Church, regional mutual aid societies, politicians, gangsters and development and demise of this Italian–American community.

Iorizzo, Luciano J. and Mondello, Salvatore. *The Italian–Americans.* New York , NY: Twayne Publishers, Inc., 1971.

Iorizzo and Mondello's study evaluates the role of the Italians in the arts, labor, business, agriculture, religion and crime in the United States. The book provides detailed approaches to such topics as Irish–American tension, the association of the Italians to the progressive movement, and the reasons for migration to America.

Johnson, Colleen Leahy. *Growing Up and Growing Old in Italian–American Families.* New Brunswick, NJ: Rutgers University Press, 1985.

Johnson's study examines the Italian–American family. This book describes and analyzes the problems between family members and how solutions are sought that need to balance personal interests and the interests of the nuclear and extended family.

Juliani, Richard N. *Building Little Italy: Philadelphia's Italians before Migration.* University Park, PA: Penn State University Press, 1998.

Juliani's work examines the Italian settlement in Philadelphia from pre–Revolution times up to the eve of mass migration in the 1870s. This book indicates that the period from the 1700s to the 1870s was important in the development of Little Italy.

Kessner, Thomas. *The Golden Door.* New York, NY: Oxford University, 1977.

Thomas Kessner's work, a study of Italians and Jews in New York City from 1880 to 1915, shows that both ethnic groups moved up the occupational ladder. The Italians, however, mostly confined their climb to blue collar work. Kessner states that the Italians considered education an unimportant continuation of one's childhood. He comments that the maintenance of this Italian attitude had the following effects on the offspring: the second generation's occupational similarity with their elders, especially in unskilled jobs; the persistence of offspring in Italian immigrant neighborhoods; the fact that the second generation did not differ much from the first generation in occupational interests; and the fact that participation in American schools made no great impact on their occupational viewpoint.

LaGumina, Salvatore J. *WOP: A Documentary History of Anti–Italian Discrimination.* Toronto, ON: Guernica, 1999 (originally published 1973).

LaGumina's volume investigates and records anti–Italian discrimination in the United States. This book demonstrates that Italians have been subject to some of the most blatant, fierce, and rough forms of discrimination to strike any group of people.

LaGumina, Salvatore J. *From Steerage to Suburbs: Long Island Italians.* Staten Island, NY: Center for Migration Studies, 1988.

LaGumina's book analyzes the social history of Italian Americans in the suburbs of Long Island. The work describes the Italian American neighborhoods in Inwood, Glen Cove, Port Washington, Westbury, Patchogue, Bellport and Copiage. It examines the early settlements, small factories, mines, farms and mansions, various forms of crime, violence, discrimination and prejudice, ethnic enclaves, changing loyalties and forging new identities of Long Island's Italian Americans.

LaGumina, Salvatore J. *The Immigrants Speak: Italian Americans Tell Their Story.* Staten Island, NY: Center for Migration Studies, 1979.

LaGumina's work records the accounts of a number of Italian Americans, from various occupations. These accounts detail the Italian American immigrant experience over the past century.

LaGumina, Salvatore J. *An Album of the Italian Americans.* New York, NY: Franklin Watts, 1972.

LaGumina's book presents an overview of the history of Italians in the United States. This work mentions some families and individuals by name.

LaGumina, Salvatore J. and Cavaioli, Frank. *The Ethnic Dimension in American Society.* Boston, MA: Holbrook Press, 1974.

LaGumina and Cavaioli, after examining the experiences of different ethnic groups (including Italian–Americans), argue that there is a maintenance of cultural diversity among the groups. They maintain that ethnicity remains as a significant factor in American society.

LaPiana, G. *The Italians in Milwaukee.* Milwaukee, WI: Associated Charities of Milwaukee, 1915.

LaPiana describes the living conditions of the Italians in Milwaukee in the early 1900s. He explains the many problems that the Italians experienced.

LaRuffa, Anthony L. *Mount Carmelo: An Italian American Community in the Bronx.* New York, NY: Gordon and Breach Science Publishers, 1988.

LaRuffa's book is a study of Little Italy in the Belmont area of the Bronx. His work describes the experiences of the Italian Americans of this community.

La Sorte, Michael. *La Merica: Images of Italian Greenhorn Experience.* Philadelphia, PA: Temple University Press, 1985.

La Sorte's book investigates the emigration of Italian men to the United States prior to the First World War from the perspective of the migrants themselves. This work describes the lives of these Italian men in Italy prior to emigration and their years in the United States.

LaValle, Kenneth (editor). *Italian Americans on Long Island: Presence and Impact.* Stony Brook, NY: Forum Italicum, 1996.

LaValle's work contains articles that examine the contributions Italian Americans have made to life on Long Island. The essays indicate that examples of the contributions of Italian–Americans on Long Island can be found in the literature and the arts, in business and labor, in education and politics.

LoGatto, Anthony F. (editor). *The Italians in America 1492–1972: A Chronology and Fact Book.* Dobbs Ferry, NY: Oceana Publications, Inc., 1972.

LoGatto's work is a compilation of documents involving Italians in America. These documents contain information on such Italians as Christopher Columbus, John Cabot, Amerigo Vespucci, Philip Mazzei, Giuseppe Garibaldi and others. The book also contains a chronology of Italians connected with key events in America history, and it includes appendices listing Italian award winners, Italian–Americans involved in business, industry, organizations, creative arts, entertaining arts, government, professions and sports.

Lopreato, Joseph. *Italian Americans.* New York, NY: Random House, 1970.

Lopreato's book describes the Americanization of Italian–Americans. This work demonstrates that the second generation Italian–American family in general and later generations exhibit behavior that is an exemplification of the social class to which it belongs. It indicates that the bulk of the Italian–American family activities occurs within the larger American society.

Lopreato, Joseph. *Peasants No More.* Scranton, PA: Chandler Publishing Co., 1967.

Lopreato's work examines the modernization of Southern Italy. This work analyzes social change in Southern Italy as an outcome of emigration.

Mangano, Antonio. *Sons of Italy: A Social and Religious Study of the Italians in America.* New York, NY: Russell and Russell, 1917.

Mangano's book describes the Italian urban community in America and Italian life in Italy. This work discusses the religious backgrounds of Italians and how the Italian can be assimilated to American life.

Mangione, Jerre. *An Ethnic at Large: A Memoir of America in the Thirties and Forties.* New York, NY: G. P. Putnam's Sons, 1978.

Mangione's book describes the difficulty that the author had in dealing with his ethnic roots in a hostile environment. This work indicates Mangione's struggles with his Italian ancestry and shows his increasing understanding that ethnicity greatly contributed to his strength of character and intellect in coping with world problems.

Mathias, Elizabeth and Raspa, Richard. *Italian Folktales in America: The Verbal Art of an Immigrant Woman.* Detroit, MI: Wayne State University Press, 1985.

Mathias and Raspa's book is a repertoire of storyteller Clementina Todesco. The book reconstructs how life was lived in a specific Italian peasant village at a particular time and place. It also explains how lore of an Italian village can be used as the baseline for a comprehension of culture changes as they influence the lives of specific villagers.

McLaughlin, Virginia, Yans. *Family and Community: Italian Immigrants in Buffalo, 1880–1930.* Ithaca, NY: Cornell University Press, 1977.

McLaughlin's text examines the lives of Italian–Americans in Buffalo, NY during the period of 1880 to 1930. This book deals with the relationship of Italian immigrants to modernization, to their adaptation in Buffalo.

Meloni, Alberto. *Italian Americans: A Study Guide and Source Book.* San Francisco, CA: R & E Research Associates, Inc., 1977.

Meloni's work is a compilation of the research, explanations and theories of numerous scholars on the Italian and Italian American experience. This book is a guide and sourcebook for Italian American studies.

Mormino, Gary Ross. *Immigrants on the Hill: Italian Americans in St. Louis, 1882–1982.* Chicago, IL: University of Illinois Press, 1986.

Mormino's book is based on extensive oral histories of the Italian Americans of the Hill, neighborhood of St. Louis from 1882 to 1982. The work focuses upon those institutions that have sustained and nurtured this Italian community. It shows how the Hill's Italian Americans have consistently encouraged ethnic pride, working class solidarity and family honor.

Musmanno, Michael A. *The Story of the Italians in America.* New York, NY: Doubleday and Company, 1965.

Musmanno's book present a sociohistorical account of the Italian–Americans. This work describes the history of Italians in America from the 16th century to the middle of the 20th century. It examines civilian life of Italians in early America, in the Ellis Island Era and during and after World War II.

Nelli, Humbert S. *From Immigrants to Ethnics: The Italian Americans.* New York, NY: Oxford University Press, 1983.

Nelli's book presents the Italian experience in the United States. This work investigates the role of Italians in the settlement of the New World and in the struggle for American independence from England. It examines the different conditions of the immigrant experience, including housing, jobs, politics, community institutions, and the family, and looks into the development of ethnic consciousness among Italian Americans.

Nelli, Humbert S. *The Italians in Chicago, 1880–1930.* New York, NY: Oxford University Press, 1970.

Nelli's work examines the Italian community in Chicago from 1880 to 1930. This book argues that Little Italy and its institutions achieved their functions, not of continuing cultural traits, brought over to Chicago from Italy, but of contributing meaningful advancements in assimilation.

Nicandri, David L. *Italians in Washington State: Emigration 1853–1924.* Tacoma, WA: The Washington State American Revolution Bicentennial Commission, 1978.

Nicandri's book describes the Italian immigrant experience in Washington State from 1852 to 1924. The work examines conditions in Italy in the nineteenth century, the Italians in the West (mostly Washington State), and the Italian immigrants on the job in Washington.

Novak, Michael. *The Rise of the Unmeltable Ethnics: Politics and Culture in the Seventies.* New York, NY: Macmillan Publishing Co., Inc., 1973.

Novak's study investigates the endurance of ethnic patterns in the United States. The book discusses the values, lie–styles, aspirations and resentments of America's millions of white ethnics (the Poles, Italians, Greeks, and Slavs). It argues that these ethnics are now a powerful force in American politics and culture.

Null, Gary and Stone, Carl. *The Italian Americans.* Harrisburg, PA: Stackpole Books, 1976.

Null and Stone's book briefly describe the lives of 600 Americans of Italian descent. It examines the contributions that these Italian Americans have made in the arts, business, entertainment, music, science, athletics, navigation, medicine, politics and journalism.

Pannunzio, Constantine M. *The Soul of an Immigrant.* New York, NY: Macmillan, 1921.

Pannunzio's book reflects on the memories of his childhood in Southern Italy. In his autobiography he describes the religious practices of Italians in Southern Italy.

Pisani, Lawrence F. *The Italian in America: A Social Study and History.* New York, NY: Exposition Press, 1957.

Pisani's book shows the part that Italians have played in American history. It demonstrates that Italian culture was no alien culture that was coming over to replace a native one, but a related culture coming to recreate old connections.

Potter, G. and Jenkins, P. *The City and the Syndicate Organizing Crime in Philadelphia.* Lexington, MA: Ginn Press, 1985.

Potter and Jenkins' work examines organized crime in Philadelphia. This book indicates that the perception of organized crime having its roots in Italy is a myth. It points out that other countries that received large numbers of Italian immigrants at the same time as the United States failed to form anything even close to the American account of the Mafia.

Putnam, Robert. *Making Democracy Work: Civic Traditions in Modern Italy.* Princeton, NJ: Princeton University Press, 1993.

Putnam examines the attitudes and the economic situation of Southern Italians in Italy during the 1970s and 1980s. He argues that in Southern Italy historical experiences shaped a culture notable for its low level of trust. The author states that this culture directly had a strong influence on Southern Italy's lack of economic development and high levels of poverty.

Reuter, Peter. *Disorganized Crime.* Cambridge, MA: MIT Press, 1983.

Reuter's book examines Italian organized crime in New York. This study indicates that no one ethnic group contrary to popular belief dominates the gambling and loan sharking businesses.

Rolle, Andrew F. *The Italian Americans: Troubled Roots.* New York, NY: The Free Press, 1980.

Rolle's book attempts to combine psychoanalysis with history in order to understand the Italian immigrants. This work looks at sexuality, the family, education, politics, religion, music, literature, the arts, food and drink, as expression of the collective need of the Italians.

Rolle, Andrew F. *The Immigrant Upraised: Italian Adventurers and Colonists in an Expanding America.* Norman, OK: University of Oklahoma Press, 1968.

Rolle's book examines the Italian immigrants' influence on the development of the United States. This work indicates that the Italians were a significant part of the labor force in the building of the railroads in the West. It provides a description on Italians in Colorado and other mining communities.

Rose, Philip M. *The Italian in America.* New York, NY: George H. Doran Co., 1922.

Rose's work examines the Italian immigrants living in the poor areas of American cities. This book describes the various problems that Italians living in tenements faced.

Sammartino, Peter (editor). *The Contributions of Italians to the United States Before the Civil War.* Washington, DC: The National Italian American Foundation, 1980.

Sammartino's work is a collection of papers on the contributions of Italians to the United States before the civil war that was sponsored by the National Italian American Foundation in Washington, DC, 1980. The book contains papers dealing with Italian contributions in literature, architecture, science, law, politics, military participation, music, art and Catholic education to America before the civil war.

Sandler, Gilbert. *The Neighborhood: The Story of Baltimore's Little Italy.* Baltimore, MD: Bodine and Associates, 1974.

Sandler's text portrays the atmosphere and history of Baltimore's Little Italy. The book gives an overall impression of the quality of life in this community. It describes this group's pressures toward and resistance against change.

Sartorio, Enrico C., *Social and Religious Life of Italians in America.* Boston, MA: Christopher Publishing House, 1918.

Sartorio's work is on the life of Italians in the United States during the period of the great migrations, the late 19th century and early 20th century. This book deals with life in the Little Italies of America. It discusses the religion of Italians and the role of churches and missions in America.

Schiavo, Giovanni, *The Italians in America before the Revolution.* New York, NY and Dallas, TX: The Vigo Press, 1976.

Schiavo explains the Italian contribution to the American colonial economic, commercial, political and cultural activities. Furthermore, twenty chapters of this book discuss the contributions made to America by such Italians as Columbus, Amerigo Vespucci, John Cabot, Giovanni Da Verrazzano, Marcos De Niza, Enrico Tonti, Alphonse Tonti, Father Bressani, Father Chino, William Paca, Philip Mazzei, Francis Vigo, Carlo Bellini, Razzolini, Ceracchi, James Philip Puglia, Giovanni Battista Saratori and Paolo Busti.

Schiavo, Giovanni, *The Truth about the Mafia and Organized Crime.* New York, NY: The Vigo Press, 1952.

Schiavo explains that organized crime in America existed before the arrival of the Italian immigrants. He also demonstrates that organized crime is not an Italian monopoly.

Schiavo, Giovanni, *Four Centuries of Italian–American History, 5 editions.* New York, NY: The Vigo Press, 1952–58.

Schiavo's work is a concise history of the Italians in America. This work deals with Italians in America from the time of Columbus to the American Revolution to the end of World War II.

Schiavo, Giovanni, *Italian American History, Vol. II.* New York, NY: The Vigo Press, 1949.

Schiavo explains the Italian contribution to the Catholic Church in America. This work chronicles the brave actions of Italian religious men and women in the United States. It also presents a history of Italian parishes in America.

Schiavo, Giovanni, *Italian American History, Vol. I.* New York, NY: The Vigo Press, 1947.

Schiavo's study discusses Italian music and musicians in America. This work contains a dictionary of music biography. It also describes the Italian–

Americans who held public office in the United States from Colonial times to the 1940s at the national, state and local levels.

Schiavo, Giovanni, *The Italians in America before the Civil War.* New York, NY: The Vigo Press, 1934.

Schiavo discusses the Italians who helped build the United States before the Civil War. The author describes the Italian influence of American culture and presents an extensive series of Italian navigators and pioneers in the United States.

Schneider, Jane and Peter. Culture *and Political Economy in Western Sicily.* New York, NY: Academic Press, 1976.

The Schneiders' text attempts to determine the specialized part that Sicily plays in historical world–systems. Their book examines Sicily's confrontation with postindustrial imperialism in the nineteenth and twentieth centuries. It describes the fate of the peasants in this encounter as Sicily moved from exporting wheat to exporting human labor.

Smith, D. *The Mafia Mystique.* New York, NY: Basic Books, 1975.

Smith's work demonstrates that the assertion that organized crime was transplanted to America from Sicily is a myth. This book argues that the importation myth of organized crime evolves from a combination of press sensationalism and native born beliefs in the United States.

Sowell, Thomas, *Ethnic America: A History.* New York, NY: Basic Books, 1981.

Sowell's book compares and contrasts the economic achievements of the different ethnic groups (including Italian–Americans) in the United States. This work argues that the principal determinant of the economic success of an ethnic group in America is the cultural traits its members brought over from their country of origin.

Stave, Bruce M., Sutherland, John F. and Salerno, Aldo. *From the Old Country: An Oral History of European Migration to America.* New York, NY: Twayne Publishers, 1994.

Stave, Sutherland and Salerno's text documents the lives of European immigrants (including Italians) in America in the immigrants' own words. This work indicates that many Americans expressed very strong negative attitudes and/or feelings toward Italians during the Great Depression.

Steinberg, Stephen, *The Ethnic Myth: Race, Ethnicity and Class in America.* Boston, MA: Beacon Press, 1981.

Steinberg's book argues that traits that are often considered ethnic may be more directly related to class, locality and other social conditions. This work investigates the economic and historical factors influencing the behavior of the various ethnic groups in America, including the Italian–Americans.

Suttles, Gerald. *Social Order of the Slum: Ethnicity and Territory in the Inner City.* Chicago, IL: University of Chicago Press, 1968.

Suttles' book is a participant observational study of Chicago's Little Italy. This work describes the attitudes, values and behaviors of the working class Italian–Americans of this community.

Thernstrom, Stephan. *The Other Bostonians: Poverty and Progress in the American Metropolis 1880–1970.* Cambridge, MA: Harvard University Press, 1973.

Thernstrom documented an occupational slipping among Irish and Italian Catholic males that he did not find with other ethnic groups. He states that Boston's first and second generation Italian and Irish Catholics who moved into white collar jobs slipped back into blue collar jobs more than the other ethnic groups studied. His main interpretation is that the cultural values of the Irish and Italians led to their dissimilar occupational patterns in comparison with the other groups.

Tomasi, Lydio. *Italian American Family.* Staten Island, NY: Center for Migration Studies, 1972.

Tomasi's work examines the Italian–American family. This book describes the changes of some major values through three generations of Italian–Americans.

Tomasi, Lydio F. (editor). *The Italian in America: The Progressive View, 1891–1914.* Staten Island, NY: Center for Migration Studies, 1978.

Tomasi's work is a collection of essays dealing with the Italians in America from 1891 to 1914. These essays describe the effect of emigration on Italy, Italian–American farmers, Italian workers of America, the Italian socialist, public health problems and economic stress of Italian–Americans, and criminality among Italian–Americans.

Tomasi, Lydio F. (editor). *Italian Americans: New Perspectives in Italian Immigration and Ethnicity.* Staten Island, NY: Center for Migration Studies, 1985.

Tomasi's volume contains the proceedings of the International Conference on the Italian Experience in the United Sates held at Columbia University, October 13–14, 1983. The papers, presented at the Conference, examine the socio-demographic profile of Italian–Americans, perceptions of Italian–Americans, and dimensions of the Italian–American experience.

Tomasi, Silvano M. *Piety and Power.* Staten Island: Center for Migration Studies, 1975.

Tomasi's book discusses three major stages in the relationship of Italian–Americans to the institutional Catholic Church in the United States. First, an effort was made to involve the Italian immigrants in the existing Irish Catholic parishes. Second, Italian parishes were developed in the United States. Third, Italian, Irish and other Catholic groups fused into a new and emerging social combination known as Middle America.

Tomasi, Silvano, M. and Stibili, Edward. *Italian Americans and Religion: An Annotated Bibliography.* Staten Island, NY: Center for Migration Studies, 1978.

Tomasi and Stibili's work is an annotated bibliography on religion in the life of Italian Americans. This annotated bibliography provides materials on the Catholic and Protestant experiences of the immigrants from Italy beginning with the period of mass immigration and going into the present.

Torrielli, Andrew J. *Italian Opinion on America, as Revealed by Italian Travelers. 1850–1900.* Cambridge, MA.: Harvard University Press, 1941.

Torrielli points out the strong interests the Italians in Italy had for America as an outcome of the stories told by Italians who had traveled to America and returned home. He indicates that economics was the chief cause of Italian migration to the United States.

Tricarico, Donald. *The Italians of Greenwich Village: The Social Structure And Transformation of an Ethnic Community.* Staten Island, NY: Center for Migration Studies, 1984.

Tricarico argues that the Italian community in Greenwich Village not only endured, but was transformed in the period following World War I. He indicates that a new form of Italian–American community organization mirrored the adaptation of the second generation to the city at a specific historical turning point.

Tyler, Gus. *Organized Crime in America.* Ann Arbor, MI: University of Michigan Press, 1962.

Tyler's book demonstrates that the roots of organized crime lie deep within American culture. This work points out that organized crime did not develop from some group of so called foreign origin (for instance, Irish, Italian, Jewish).

Varacalli, Joseph, Primeggia, Salvatore, LaGumina, Salvatore J. and D'Elia, Donald J., (editors). *The Saints in the Lives of Italian–Americans: An Interdisciplinary Investigation.* New York, NY: Forum Italicum, Inc., 1999.

Varacalli, Primeggia, LaGumina, and D'Elia's book is a collection of original essays on Italian–American religious life. This work provides sociological, historical, psychological, philosophical and theological explanations on Italian–Americans' devotion to the saints.

Ware, Caroline. *Greenwich Village, 1920–1930.* New York, NY: Harper and Row, 1965.

Ware's study examines the life of Italian–Americans in Greenwich Village in the 1920s. This work gives emphasis to the breakdown of traditional family patterns and paesani loyalties as the second generation Italian–Americans obtained American customs. It concludes that Italian–Americans in the Village were a traditionless and disorganized group.

Wechman, Robert, J. *The Economic Development of the Italian–American.* Champaign, IL: Stipes Publishing Company, 1983.

Wechman's book examines the economics of the Italians in the United States from the early explorers to the 20th century. This work points out the contribution of Italian mutual benefit organizations to the economic development of the Italian immigrant.

Weibust, Patricia Snyder, Capobianco, Gennaro, and Gould, Sally Innis, *The Italians: In Their Homeland, In America, In Connecticut.* Storrs, CT: The Peoples of Connecticut Multicultural Ethnic Heritage Series, 1976.

Weibust, Capobianco and Gould's book presents information on the sociocultural background of the Italian immigrants and the Italian–Americans in Connecticut. This work presents a brief history of Italy. It discusses the education, language, literature, gestures, music, religion, beliefs and family of the Italians in Italy. Moreover, the book examines the history, family, occupations, religion, folk beliefs, social organizations, education and politics of the Italian–Americans in Connecticut.

Whyte, William Foote. *Street Corner Society.* Chicago, IL: University of Chicago Press, 1943.

Whyte's study examines the lives of Italian–Americans in Little Italy in Boston's North End during the late 1930s to the early 1940s. The book describes the social structure of this Little Italy. It points out the nature and problems of Boston's North End.

Williams, Phyllis H. *South Italian Folkways in Europe and America: A Handbook for Social Workers, Visiting Nurses, School Teachers, and Physicians.* New York, NY: Russell and Russell, 1938.

Williams' work is a concise handbook on the socio–anthropological context of the Italian sub communities in America from the 1890s to the 1930s. This book examines the cultural problems that the Italian immigrants face in adjusting to life in America. It describes the folkways, mores and institutions that define the Italian way of life.

Workings of the Federal Writers' Project, Works Progress Administration in the City of New York. *The Italians of New York.* New York, NY: Arno Press and the New York Times, 1969.

This book by the Federal Writers' Project examines the Italian American experience in New York City from the 1870s to the 1930s. The work investigates the causes of Italian migration to New York City, and the work experiences, religious, social, intellectual and cultural life of the Italians in the city.

NOTES

1. Originally published in *Voices in Italian Americana Internet Site,* 2005.

BIBLIOGRAPHY

Abadinsky, Howard. *Organized Crime.* Chicago, IL: Nelson Hall, 1985.

Abramson, Harold. J. *Ethnic Diversity in Catholic America.* New York, NY: John Wiley and Sons, 1973.

Alba, Richard. *Italian Americans into the Twilight of Ethnicity.* Englewood Cliffs, NJ: Prentice–Hall, 1985.

Alfano, M. "Negative Stereotypes Persist Though FBI Figures Reveal Facts." *ComUnico Magazine,* April 2002.

American Italian Historical Association Publications of Proceedings. Staten Island, NY: American Italian Historical Association, Volumes 1 to 30 from 1968 to 1999.

Volume 1 *Ethnicity in American Political Life: The Italian American Case.* Edited by Salvatore J. LaGumina (1968).

Volume 2 *The Italian American Novel.* Edited by John M. Cammett (1969).

Volume 3 *An Inquiry into Organized Crime.* Edited by Luciano J. Iorizzo (1970).

Volume 4 *Power and Class: The Italian American Experience Today.* Edited by Frances X. Femminella (1971).

Volume 5 *Italian American Radicalism: Old World Origins and New World Developments.* Edited by Rudolph J. Vecoli (1972).

Volume 6 *The Religious Experience of Italian Americans.* Edited by Silvano Tomasi (1973).

Volume 7 *The Interaction of Italians and Jews in America.* Edited by Jean Scarpaci (1974).

Volume 8 *The Urban Experience of Italian Americans.* Edited by Pat Gallo (1975).

Volume 9 *The United States and Italy: The First Two Hundred Years.* Edited by Humbert Nelli (1976).

Volume 10 *The Italian Immigrant Woman in North America.* Edited by Betty Boyd Caroli, Robert Harney, and Lydio F. Tomasi (1977).

Volume 11 *Pane e Lavoro: The Italian American Working Class.* Edited by George E. Pozzetta (1978).

Volume 12 *Italian Americans in the Professions.* Edited by Remegio U. Pane (1983).

Volume 13 *The Family and Community Life of Italian Americans.* Edited by Richard Juliani (1983).

Volume 14 *Italian Immigrants in Rural and Small Town America.* Edited by Rudolph J. Vecoli (1987).

Volume 15 *The Italian Americans Through the Generations: The First One Hundred Years.* Edited by Rocco Caporale (1986).

Volume 16 *The Interaction of Italians and Irish in the United States.* Edited by Francis X. Femminella (1985).

Volume 17 *Italian Americans: Struggle and Support.* Edited by Joseph L. Tropea, James E. Miller, and Cheryl Beattie Repetti (1986).

Volume 18 *The Melting Pot and Beyond: Italian Americans in the Year 2000.* Edited by Jerome Krase and William Egelman (1987).

Volume 19 *Italian Americans: The Search for a Usable Past.* Edited by Richard Juliani and Philip V. Cannistraro (1989).

Volume 20 *Italian Ethnics: Their Languages, Literature and Life.* Edited by Dominic Candeloro, Fred Gardaphe, and Paolo Giordano (1990).

Volume 21 *Italian Americans in Transition.* Edited by Joseph Scelsa, Salvatore J. LaGumina, and Lydio F. Tomasi (1990).

Volume 22 *Italian Americans Celebrate Life.* Edited by Paola A. Sensi Isolani andAn-
thony Julian Tamburri (1990).
Volume 23 *A Century of Italian Immigration, 1890–1990.* Edited by Harral Landry
(1994).
Volume 24 *Italian Americans and Their Public and Private Life.* Edited by Frank
J.Cavaioli, Angela Danzi, and Salvatore J. LaGumina (1993).
Volume 25 *New Explorations in Italian American Studies.* Edited by Richard Juliani. and
Sandra P. Juliani (1994).
Volume 26 *Italian Americans in a Multicultural Society.* Edited by Jerome Krase and
Judith N. DeSena (1994).
Volume 27 *Through the Looking Glass: Italian and Italian/American Images in theMe-
dia.* Edited by Mary Jo Bona and Anthony Julian Tamburri (1996).
Volume 28 *Industry, Technology, Labor and the Italian American Communities.* Edited
by Mario Aste, Jerome Krase, Louise Napolitano–Carman and Janet E. Worrall
(1997).
Volume 29 *A Tavola: Food, Tradition and Community among Italian Americans.* Edited
by Edvige Giunta and Sam Patti (1998).
Volume 30 *Shades of Black and White Conflict and Collaboration between Two Commu-
nities.* Edited by Dan Ashyk, Fred L. Gardaphe and Anthony Julian Tamburri
(1999).
Americans of Italian Descent: A Study of Public Images, Beliefs and Misperceptions.
Washington, DC: The National Public Opinion Research for Commission for Social
Justice Order Sons of Italy, 1991.
Amfitheatrof, Erik. *The Children of Columbus: An Informal History of the Italians in the
New World.* Boston, MA: Little, Brown and Company, 1973.
Balboni, Alan R. *Beyond the Mafia: Italian Americans and the Development of Las Vega.*
Reno, NV: University of Nevada Press, 1996.
Banfield, Edward C. *The Moral Basis of a Backward Society.* New York, NY: The Free
Press,1958.
Barzini, Luigi. *The Italians.* New York: Atheneum Publishes, 1964.
Battistella, Graziano (editor). *Italian Americans in the 80s: A Sociodemographic Profile.*
Staten Island, NY: Center for Migration Studies, 1989.
Bell, Rudolph B. *Fate and Honor, Family and Village: Demographic and Cultural
Change in Rural Italy Since 1800.* Chicago, IL: University of Chicago Press, 1979.
Belliotti, Raymond A. *Seeking Identity: Individualism versus Community in an Ethnic
Context.* Lawrence, KS: University Press of Kansas, 1995.
Biagiotti, Aldo P. *Impact: The Historical Account of the Italian Immigrants of Ridgefield
Connecticut.* Ridgefield, CT: Ronald Press, 1990.
Bianco, Carla. *The Two Rosetos.* Bloomington, IN: Indiana University Press, 1974.
Blau, Peter. M. and Duncan, Otis. D., *The American Occupational Structure.* New York,
NY: Wiley, 1967.
Block, Anton. *The Mafia of a Sicilian Village, 1860–1960.* Prospect Heights, IL: Waveland
Press, 1971.
Block, A. and Scarpitti, F. *Poisoning for Profit: The Mafia and Toxic Waste.* New York,
NY: William Morrow, 1985.
Bohme, Frederick. G. *A History of the Italians in New Mexico.* New York, NY: Arno
Press, 1975.
Briggs, John W. *An Italian Passage: Immigrants to Three American Cities 1870–1930.* New
Haven, CT: Yale University, 1978.

Broom, L. Martin, C. A. and Maynard, B."Status Profiles of Racial and Ethnic Populations." Paper read at the meetings of the Pacific Sociological Association, Long Beach, CA, 1967.

Browne, Malcolm W. "A Look at Success of Young Asians." *New York Times*, March 25, 1986.

Bruhn, John G. and Wolf, Stewart. *The Roseto Story: An Anatomy of Health.* Norman, OK: University of Oklahoma Press, 1979.

Buhle, Paul and Georgakas, Dan (editors). *The Immigrant Left in the United States.* Albany, NY: State University Press, 1997.

Capozzola, Richard A. *Finalmente: The Truth about Organized Crime.* Altamonte Springs, FL: Five Centuries Books, 2001.

Caso, Adolfo. *"Giovanni Schiavo: Father of Italian–American* History." *Buon Giorno*, August 1998.

Cauchon, D. "Head of BCCI–linked Bank Quits." *USA Today*, August 15, 1991.

Chambliss, William. *On the Take: From Petty Crooks to Presidents.* Bloomington, IN: Indiana University Press, 1978.

Child, Irvin. Italian or American? The Second Generation in Conflict. New Haven, CT: Yale University, 1943.

Churchill, Charles W. *The Italians of Newark: A Community Study.* New York, NY: Arno Press, 1975.

Cinel, Dino, *From Italy to San Francisco: The Immigrant Experience.* Palo Alto, California: Stanford University Press, 1982.

Colleta, John Philip. *Finding Italian Roots.* Baltimore, MD: Genealogical Publishing Co., Inc., 1993.

Cordasco, Francesco. *Italian Americans: A Guide to Information Sources.* Detroit, MI: Gale ResearchCo., 1978.

Cordasco, Francesco (editor). *Studies in Italian American Social History: Essays in Honor of Leonard Covello.* Totora, New Jersey: Rowman and Littlefield, 1975.

Cordasco, Francesco and Bucchioni, Eugene (editors). *The Italians: Social Backgrounds of an American Group.* Clifton, NJ: Augustus M. Kelley Publishers, 1974.

Covello, Leonard. *The Sociological Background of the Italo American School Child.* Leiden, Netherlands: E.J. Brill, 1967.

Crispino, James. *The Assimilation of Ethnic Groups: The Italian Case.* Staten Island, NY: Center for Migration Studies, 1980.

Cronin, Constance. *The Sting of Change: Sicilians in Sicily and Australia.* Chicago, IL: University of Chicago Press, 1970.

Dal Cerro, Bill. *Italian Culture on Film 1928–1999.* Floral Park, NY: Italic Studies Institute Image Research Project, 1999.

Davis, J. "Morals and Backwardness." *Comparative Studies in Society and History 12,* 1970.

Del Guidice, Luisa (editor). *Studies in Italian American Folklore.* Logan, UT: Utah StatePress, 1993.

DeMarco, William M. *Ethnics and Enclaves: Boston's Italian North End.* Ann Harbor, MI: UMI Research Press, 1981.

Di Franco, Philip. *The Italian American Experience.* New York, NY: Tom Doherty Associates, 1988.

Diggins, John P. *Mussolini and Fascism: The View from America.* Princeton, NJ: Princeton University Press, 1972.

DiNovo, Philip .J. "Giovanni Schiavo, Author and Historian." *Il Popolo Italiano, October,* 1989.

Dolci, Danilo. *Sicilian Lives.* New York, NY: Pantheon Books, 1981.

Egelman, William S. "Italian and Irish Americans in Education: A Sociohistoric Analysis." In F. X. Femminella (editor). *Italians and Irish in America.* Staten Island, NY: American Italian Historical Association, 1985.

Fucilla, Joseph G. *Our Italian Surnames.* Baltimore: Genealogical Publishing Co., Inc., 1987.

Gallo, Patrick J. *Ethnic Alienation: The Italian–Americans.* Rutherford, N.J.: Fairleigh Dickinson University Press, 1974.

——. *Old Bread, New Wine: A Portrait of the Italian–Americans.* Chicago, IL: Nelson Hall, 1981.

Gambino, Richard. *Blood of My Blood.* Garden City, NY: Doubleday and Company, 1974.

——. *Vendetta: The Story of the Largest Lynching in American History,* Garden City, NY: Doubleday, 1977.

——. "America's Most Tolerated Intolerance: Bigotry against Italian Americans."*The Italian American Review,* Spring/Summer, 1997.

Gans, Herbert. *The Urban Villagers: Group and Class in the Life of Italian–Americans.* New York, NY: The Free Press, 1962.

Gelorimino, A., Gerald and Gotti, Margaret R. *The Italian Heritage in Yonkers.* Yonkers, NY: Gazette Press, Inc., Publishers, 1986.

Gesualdi, Louis. *The Italian Immigrants of Connecticut, 1880 to 1940.* New Haven, CT: Connecticut Academy of Arts and Sciences, 1997.

——. *Italian American Studies: A Guide.* Global Research Monograph Series, No. 11, Center for Global Education, Jamaica, NY: St. John's University, March 1999.

——. "Giovanni Schiavo's Works: A Summary." *ComUnico Magazine,* February 2000.

——."An Inaccurate Notion of Southern Italy." *ComUnico Magazine,* June, 2000.

——."Bruhn and Wolf's Study of Roseto, Pennsylvania: A Brief Discussion." *ComUnico Magazine,* October, 2000.

——."Praises for Giovanni Schiavo." *ComUnico Magazine,* October, 2000.

——."Some Ideas for Italian/American Research." Presented at *The Italian American Experience in the New York City Area Conference,* St. John's University Italian Cultural Center, Jamaica, NY, September 28, 2001.

——. *A Reply to the Moral Basis of a Backward Society.* New York, NY: John D. Calandra Topical Issues Series of City University of New York, 2001.

——. *The Cultural Trait Approach: A Critique,* New York, NY: John D. Calandra Topical Issues Series of City University of New York, 2001.

——. "The Italian American Experience: An Annotated Bibliography." *Voices in Italian Americana Internet Site,* 2005.

——."*Making Democracy Work:* Criticisms and Response." In Jerome Krase, Philip Cannistraro and Joseph Scelsa (editors). *Italian American Politics: Local, Global/Cultural, Personal.* New York, NY: American Italian Historical Association, 2005.

——."Popular Held Beliefs about Italian Americans and Organized Crime." Unpublished paper, 2006.

Giordano, Joseph (editor).*The Italian–American Catalog: A Lavish and Loving Celebration of and Guide to Our Culture, History, Neighborhoods, Family, Food and Drink.* New York, NY: Doubleday and Company, Inc., 1986.

Giovanni Schiavo Collection. Research Library of the American Italian Renaissance Foundation. New Orleans, Louisiana.

Glazer, Nathan. *Ethnic Dilemmas, 1964–1982.* Cambridge, MA: Harvard University Press, 1983.

——. *The New Immigration: A Challenge to American Society.* San Diego, CA: San Diego State University Press, 1988.

——. *The Limits of Social Policy.* Cambridge, MA: Harvard University Press, 1988.

Glazer, Nathan and Moynihan, Daniel P. *Beyond the Melting Pot.* Cambridge, MA: The M.I.T. Press, 1971.

Gordon, Milton M. *Assimilation in American Life.* New York, NY: Oxford University Press, 1964.

Gramsci, Antonio. *The Southern Question.* Toronto, ON: Guernica Editions, Inc., 1995.

Grande, Albert, "The Cultural and Intellectual Experience of Italian–Americans: Some Observations." In Humbert Nelli (editor). *The United States and Italy: The First Two Hundred Years.* Staten Island, New York: American Italian Historical Association, 1977.

——."The Intellectual Image of Italian–Americans." *Unico Magazine,* Vol. 35, No. 5, 1980.

Graubard, Stephen G. "Why Do Asian Pupils Win These Prizes?" *New York Times,* January19, 1988.

Greeley, Andrew M. *Why Can't They Be Like Us? : America's White Ethnic Groups.* New York, NY: Dutton, 1971.

——. *Ethnicity in the United States.* New York, NY: Wiley, 1974.

——. *The American Catholic: A Social Portrait.* New York, NY: Basic Books, Inc., 1977.

——. *The Irish Americans: The Rise to Money and Power.* New York, NY: Harper and Row, Publishers, 1981.

——. *The Catholic Myth: The Behavior and Beliefs of American Catholics.* New York, NY: MacMillan Publishers, Company, 1990.

Greeley, Andrew M and McCready, William C. "The Transmission of Culture Heritages: The Case of the Irish and the Italians." In Nathan Glazer and Daniel P. Moynihan (editors). *Ethnicity.* Cambridge, MA: Harvard University Press, 1975.

Grossman, Ronald P. *The Italians in America,* Minneapolis. MN: Lerner Publications, 1975.

Gumina, Deanna Paoli. *The Italians in San Francisco (1850–1930).* Staten Island, NY: Center for Migration Studies, 1977.

Harney, Robert F. and Scarpaci, J. Vincenza (editors). *Little Italies in North America.* Toronto. ON: The Multicultural History Society of Ontario, 1981.

Healey, J. *Race, Ethnicity and Gender in the United States: Inequality, Group Conflict and Power.* Thousand Oaks, CA: Pine Forge Press, 1997.

Ianni, Francis A. J. *A Family Business.* New York, NY: Mentor, 1972.

Immerso, Michael. *Newark's Little Italy: The Vanished First Ward.* New Brunswick, N.J.: Rutgers University Press, 1997.

Iorrizo, Luciano J., and Mondello, Salvatore. *The Italian–Americans.* New York, NY: Twayne Publishers, Inc., 1971.

Johnson, Colleen Leahy. *Growing Up and Growing Old in Italian–American Families.* New Brunswick, N.J: Rutgers University Press, 1985.

Juliani, Richard N. *Building Little Italy: Philadelphia's Italians before Migration.* University Park, Pennsylvania: Penn State University Press, 1998.

Kappeler, V., Blumberg, M. and Potter, G. *The Mythology of Crime and Criminal Justice.* Prospect Heights, Illinois: Waveland Press, 2000.

Kessner, Thomas. *The Golden Door.* New York, NY: Oxford University, 1977.

Kroeber, Alfred. *Anthropology.* New York, NY: Harcourt Jovanovich, 1948.

Kroeber, Alfred and Parsons, Talcott. "The Concept of Culture and of Social Systems." *American Sociological Review,* 23, 1958.

LaGumina, Salvatore. *An Album of the Italian American.* New York, NY: Franklin Watts, 1972.

——. *The Immigrants Speak: Italian Americans Tell Their Story.* Staten Island, NY: Center for Migration Studies, 1979.

——. *From Steerage to Suburbs: Long Island Italians.* Staten Island, NY: Center for Migration Studies, 1988.

——. *WOP: A Documentary History of Anti–Italian Discrimination.* Toronto: Guernica, 1999 (originally published 1973).

LaGumina, Salvatore and Cavaioli Frank. *The Ethnic Dimension in American Society.* Boston, A: Holbrook Press, 1974.

LaPiana, G. *The Italians in Milwaukee,* Milwaukee. WI: Associated Charities of Milwaukee, 1915,

LaRuffa, A. L., *Mount Carmelo: An Italian American Community in the Bronx.* New York, NY: Gordon and Breach Science Publishers, 1988.

La Sorte, Michael. *La Merica: Images of Italian Greenhorn Experience.* Philadelphia, PA: Temple University Press, 1985.

LaValle, Kenneth (editor). *Italian Americans on Long Island: Presence and Impact.* Stony Brook, NY: Forum Italicum, 1996.

Lichter, S. Robert, and Amundson, Daniel R. *Portrayal of Italian American Characters in Prime Television Series, 1994–1995.* Washington, DC: Social Justice Order Sons of Italy in America, 1996.

LoGatto, Anthony F. (editor). *The Italians in America 1492–1972: A Chronology and Fact Book.* Dobbs Ferry, New York: Oceana Publications, Inc., 1972

Lopreato, Joseph. *Peasants No More.* Scranton, Pennsylvania: Chandler Publishing Co., 1967.

——. *Italian Americans.* New York, NY: Random House, 1970.

Lujinnos, Carol C. "The Only Real Indian is the Stereotyped Indian." In Coramae Richey Mann and Marjorie S. Zatz (editors). *Images of Color Images of Crime.* Los Angeles, CA: Roxbury Publishing Co., 1998.

Mangano, Antonio. *Sons of Italy: A Social and Religious Study of Italians in America.* New York, NY: Russell and Russell, 1917.

Mangione, Jerre, *An Ethnic at Large: A Memoir of America in the Thirties and Forties.* New York, NY: E. P. Putnam's Sons, 1978.

Mannin, M. L. "European Politics–*Making Democracy Work.*" *Political Studies.*September 1994, p. 533.

Maraffi, Marco. "Review of *Making Democracy Work.*" *American Journal of Sociology,* March 1994, pp. 1348–1349.

Mathias, Elizabeth and Raspa, Richard. *Italian Folktales in America: The Verbal Art of an Immigrant Woman.* Detroit, MI: Waynes State University Press, 1985.

McCorkel, Thomas. "Review of *The Moral Basis of a Backward Society* by E.C. Banfield." *American Anthropologist,* 61, 1959.

McLaughlin, Virginia Yans, *Family and Community: Italian Immigrants in Buffalo, 1880–1930.* Ithaca: NY: Cornell University Press, 1977.

Meloni, Alberto, *Italian Americans: A Study Guide and Source Book.* San Francisco, CA: R & E Research Associates, Inc., 1977.

Mills, J. *The Underground Empire: Where Crime and Government Embrace.* New York, NY: Doubleday, 1986.

Mormino, Gary Ross. *Immigrants on the Hill: Italian Americans in St. Louis, 1882–1982.* Chicago, IL: University of Illinois Press, 1986.

Moss, Leonard W. "The Family in Southern Italy: Yesterday and Today." In H.S. Nelli (editor). *The United States and Italy: The First Two Hundred Years.* Staten Island, NY: American Italian Historical Association, 1977.

Muraskin, William. "The Moral Basis of a Backward Sociologist: Edward Banfield, the Italians and the Italian Americans." *American Journal of Sociology, 20,* 1974.

Musmanno, Michael A. *The Story of Italians in America.* New York, NY: Doubleday andCompany, 1965,

Nelli, Humbert S. *The Italians in Chicago, 1880–1930.* New York, NY: Oxford University Press, 1970.

Nicandri, David L. *Italians in Washington State: Emigration, 1853–1924.* Tacoma, WA: The Washington State American Revolution Bicentennial Commission, 1978.

Novak, Michael. *The Rise of the Unmeltable Ethnics: Politics and Culture in the Seventies.* New York, NY: Macmillan Publishing Co., Inc., 1973.

Null, Gary and Stone, Carl. *The Italian Americans.* Harrisburg, PA: Stackpole Books, 1976.

Oxnam, Robert B. "Why Asians Succeed Here." *New York Times Magazine,* November 20, 1986.

Pannunzio, Constantine M. *The Soul of an Immigrant.* New York, NY: Macmillan, 1921.

Parsons, Talcott. *The Social System.* Glencoe, ILL: Free Press, 1951.

——. "Sociological Theory." *Encyclopedia Britannica 20,* 1067.

——. "On Building Social System Theory: A Personal History." *Daedalus* 99, 1970.

Peabody, N.S. "Toward an Understanding of Backwardness and Change: A Critique of the Banfield Hypothesis." *The Journal of Developing Areas, 4,* 1970.

Pisani, Lawrence F. *The Italian in America: A Social Study and History.* New York. NY: Exposition Press, 1957.

Potter, G. and Jenkins, P. *The City and the Syndicate Organizing Crime in Philadelphia.* Lexington, MA: Ginn Press, 1985.

Putnam, Robert D. *Making Democracy Work: Civic Traditions in Modern Italy.* Princeton, NJ: Princeton University Press, 1993.

Reuter, Peter. *Disorganized Crime.* Cambridge, MA: MIT Press, 1983.

Rolle, Andrew F. *The Italian Americans: Troubled Roots.* New York, NY: The Free Press, 1980.

——. *The Immigrant Upraised: Italian Adventurers and Colonists in an Expanding America.* Norman, OK: University of Oklahoma Press, 1968.

Rose, Philip M. *The Italian in America.* New York, NY: George H. Doran Co., 1922.

Rosen, Bernard, C."Race, Ethnicity and the Achievement Syndrome." *American Sociological Review 24,* 1959.

Rosoff, Stephen M., Pontell, Henry N. and Tillman, Robert H. *Profit without Honor: White–Collar Crime and the Looting of America.* Upper Saddle River, NJ: Pearson Education, Inc., 2002.

Salamone, Frank, A. "Moral Familism: Italian–Americans and Societa." In R.N. Juliani and S. P. Juliani (editors). *New Explorations in Italian American Studies.* Staten Island, NY: American Italian Historical Association, 1994.

Sammartino, Peter. *Italian American Digest,* Summer, 1983.

—— (editor). *The Contributions of Italians to the United States Before the Civil War.* Washington D. C.: The National Italian American Foundation, 1980.

Sandler, Gilbert. *The Neighborhood: The Story of Baltimore's Little Italy.* Baltimore, MD: Bodine and Associates, 1974.

Sartorio, Enrico C. *Social and Religious Life of Italians in America.* Boston, MA: Christopher Publishing House, 1918.

Schappes, Morris U. "Review of Nathan Glazer's American Judaism." *Journal of Ethnic Studies,* Fall, 1973.

Schiavo, Giovanni. *The Italians in America before the Civil War.* New York, NY The Vigo Press, 1934.

——. *Italian American History, Vol. I.* New York, NY: The Vigo Press, 1947.

——. *Italian American History, Vol. II.* New York, NY: The Vigo Press, 1949.

——. *The Truth about the Mafia and Organized Crime.* New York, NY: The Vigo Press, 1952.

——. *Four Centuries of Italian–American History,* 5 editions. New York, NY: The Vigo Press, 1952–58.

——. *The Italians in America before the Revolution.* New York, NY and Dallas, TX: The Vigo Press, 1976.

Schneider, Jane and Schneider, Peter. *Culture and Political Economy in Western Sicily.* New York, NY: Academic Press, 1976.

Shils, Edward. *Tradition.* Chicago, IL: The University of Chicago Press, 1981.

Silverman, Sydel F. "Agricultural Organization, Social Structure and Values in Italy: Amoral Familism Reconsidered." *American Anthropologist 21,* 1968.

Simon, David R. *Elite Deviance.* Boston, MA: Allyn and Bacon, 1999.

Smith, D. *The Mafia Mystique.* New York, NY: Basic Books, 1975.

Sorrentino, Anthony. *Organizing the Ethnic Community.* Staten Island, NY: Center for Migration Studies, 1995.

Sowell, Thomas. *Ethnic America: A History.* New York, NY: Basic Books, 1981.

——. *Is Reality Optional?* Paolo Alto, CA: Hoover Institute Press, 1993

——. *Migration and Cultures: A World View.* New York, NY: Basic Books, 1996.

Stark, Rodney. *Sociology.* Belmont, CA: Wadsworth Publishing Co., 1985.

Steinberg, Stephen. *The Ethnic Myth,* Boston. MA: Beacon Press, 1989.

——. *Turning Back: The Retreat From Racial Justice: An American Thought and Policy.* Boston: Beacon Press, 1995.

Stone, Frank. *The Irish of Connecticut.* Storrs, CT: Ethnic Heritage Studies Series, 1975.

Strodtbeck. Fred L. "Family Interaction, Values and Achievement." In Sklare, Marshall (editor). *The Jews: Social Patterns of an American Group.* New York, NY: Free Press, 1958.

Suttles, Gerald D. *The Social Order of a Slum: Ethnicity and Territory in the Inner City.* Chicago, IL: University of Chicago Press, 1968.

Thernstrom, Stephen. *The Other Bostonians: Poverty and Progress in the American Metropolis, 1880–1970.* Cambridge, MA: Harvard University Press, 1973.

Tomasi, Lydio F. *Italian American Family.* Staten Island, NY: Center for Migration Studies, 1972.

—— (editor). *The Italian in America: The Progressive View, 1891–1914.* Staten Island, NY: Center for Migration Studies, 1978.

—— (editor). *Italian Americans: New Perspectives in Italian Immigration and Ethnicity.* Staten Island, NY: Center for Migrations Studies, 1985.

Tomasi, Silvano M. *Piety and Power.* Staten Island: Center for Migration Studies, 1975.

Tomasi, Silvano M. and Stibili, Edward. *Italian Americans and Religion: An Annotated Bibliography.* New York: Center for Migration Studies, 1978.

Torrielli, Andrew J. *Italian Opinion on America as Revealed by Italian Travelers, 1850–1900.* Cambridge, MA: Harvard University Press, 1941.

Tricarico, Donald. *The Italians of Greenwich Village: The Social Structure and Transformation of an Ethnic Community.* Staten Island, NY: Center for Migration Studies, 1984.

Tumin, Melvin, E. *Patterns of Society.* Boston, MA: Little Brown, 1973.

Tyler, Gus. *Organized Crime in America*. Ann Arbor, MI: University of Michigan Press, 1962.

Urbinati, Nadia. "The Art of Tolerance–*Making Democracy Work." Dissent Fall*, 1993.

Varacalli, Joseph, Primeggia, Salvatore, LaGumina, Salvatore J., and D'Elia, Donald J. (editors). *The Saints in the Lives of Italian–Americans: An Interdisciplinary Investigation*. New York, NY: Forum Italicum, Inc., 1999.

Ware, Caroline. *Greenwich Village, 1920–1930*. New York, NY: Harper and Row, 1965.

Wechman, Robert J. *The Economic Development of the Italian–American*. Champaign, IL: Stipes Publishing Company, 1983.

Weibust, Patricia S. Capobianco, Gennaro and Gould, Sally Innis. *The Italians; In Their Homeland, In America, In Connecticut*. Storrs, CT: The Peoples of Connecticut Multicultural Ethnic Heritage Series, 1976.

Whyte, William Foote. *Street Corner Society*. Chicago, IL: University of Chicago Press, 1943.

Williams, Phyllis H. *South Italian Folkways in Europe and America: A Handbook for Social Workers , Visiting Nurses, School Teachers and Physicians*. New York, NY: Russell and Russell, 1938.

Wolfe, Anna C. "The Invisible Jewish Poor." In N. Levine and M. Hochbaum (editors). *Poor Jews*. New Brunswick, N J: Transaction Books, 1974.

Workings of the Federal Writers' Project, Works Progress Administration in the City of New York. *The Italians of New York*. New York, NY: Arno Press and the New York Times, 1969.

Zogby International. *National Survey: American Teenagers and Stereotyping*. Utica, NY: Zogby International, 2001.

INDEX

Femminella, Francis X., 51, 56
Fucilla, Joseph G., 64

Gallo, Patrick J., 57, 64
Gambino, Richard, 6, 13–14, 15, 17, 29, 51, 64–65
Gans, Herbert, 3, 65
Gardaphe, Fred, 51
Gelorimino, A. Gerald and Gotti, Margaret R., 65
Gesualdi, Louis, 22, 51, 65
Giordano, Joseph, 65–66
Giunto, Edvige and Patti, Sam, 58
Glazer, Nathan, 14, 16, 66
Glazer, Nathan and Moynihan, Daniel P., 13, 14, 66
Gordon, Milton M., 13, 14
Gramsci, Antonio, 1–2
Grande, Albert, 19
Graubard, Stephen C., 16
Greeley, Andrew, 14, 16, 66–67
Greeley, Andrew and McCready, William, 13, 15
Grossman, Ronald P., 67
Gumina, Deanna Paoli, 67

Harney, Robert and Scarpaci, J. Vicenza, 67
Healey J., 22

Ianni, Francis A. J., 67
Immerso, Michael, 67
Iorizzo, Luciano J., 51, 56
Iorizzo, Luciano J. and Mondello, Salvatore, 68
Isolani, Paola A. Sensi, 52
Isolani, Paola A. Sensi and Tamburri, Anthony Julian, 58
Italian Americana, 47
Italian/American journals, 45–49
Italian American Review, 47
Italian American Organizations, 45–49
Italian American Research, 41–43
Italian American Scholars, 49–54
Italian/American Studies, 45–54
Italian Cultural Center, 47
Italian immigration, 20–22

Johnson, Colleen Leahy, 68
Juliani, Rchard N., 52, 57, 68
Juliani, Richard N. and Canninstraro, Philip V. 57
Juliani, Richard N. and Juliani, Sandra P. 58

Kappeler, V., Blumberg, M. and Potter, G., 29
Kessner, Thomas, 14, 15, 68
Krase, Jerome, 52
Krase, Jerome and DeSenna, Judith N., 58
Krase, Jerome and Egelman, William, 57
Kroeber, Alfred, 13
Kroeber, Alfred and Parsons, Talcott, 13

LaGumina, Salvatore, 52, 68–69
LaGumina, Salvatore and Cavaioli, Frank, 13–14, 15, 69
Landry, Harral, 58
LaPiana, G., 69
LaSorte, Michael, 70
LaValle, Kenneth, 70
Lichter, S. Robert and Amundon, Daniel R., 27
LoGatto, Anthony F., 70
Lopreato, Joseph 4, 17, 18, 19, 20, 52, 70
Lujinnos, Carol Chingo, 30

Mafia, 27, 28, 29, 30
Mangano, Antonio, 71
Mangione, Jerre, 71
Mannin, M. L., 9–10
Maraffi, Marco, 10
Marchione, Margherita, 52
Mathias, Elizabeth, 53
Mathias, Elizabeth and Raspa, Richard, 71
McCorkel, Thomas, 4
McLaughlin, Virginia Yans, 71
Meloni, Alberto, 71
Milione, Vincenzo, 53
Mills, J., 29
Mormino, Gary Ross, 71–72
Moss, Leonard W., 5–6

CPSIA information can be obtained at www.ICGtesting.com
Printed in the USA
BVOW062219030512

289299BV00003B/3/P